P9-DMG-918

WHEN A *Woman* INSPIRES HER HUSBAND

Cindi McMenamin

HARVEST HOUSE PUBLISHERS

EUGENE, OREGON

Unless otherwise indicated, all Scripture quotations are from The Holy Bible, *New International Version*® *NIV*®. Copyright © 1973, 1978, 1984, 2011 by Biblica, Inc.™ Used by permission. All rights reserved worldwide.

Verses marked NASB are taken from the New American Standard Bible®, © 1960, 1962, 1963, 1968, 1971, 1972, 1973, 1975, 1977, 1995 by The Lockman Foundation. Used by permission. (www.Lockman.org)

Verses marked MSG are taken from The Message. Copyright © by Eugene H. Peterson 1993, 1994, 1995, 1996, 2000, 2001, 2002. Used by permission of NavPress Publishing Group.

Verses marked NLT are taken from the *Holy Bible,* New Living Translation, copyright © 1996, 2004. Used by permission of Tyndale House Publishers, Inc., Wheaton, IL 60189 USA. All rights reserved.

Verses marked CEV are taken from the Contemporary English Version © 1991, 1992, 1995 by American Bible Society. Used with permission.

Cover by Left Coast Design, Portland, Oregon

Cover photo © iStockphoto / LindaYolanda

WHEN A WOMAN INSPIRES HER HUSBAND
Copyright © 2011 by Cindi McMenamin
Published by Harvest House Publishers
Eugene, Oregon 97402
www.harvesthousepublishers.com

Library of Congress Cataloging-in-Publication Data
McMenamin, Cindi, 1965-
When a woman inspires her husband / Cindi McMenamin.
  p. cm.
Includes bibliographical references.
ISBN 978-0-7369-2948-6 (pbk.)
ISBN 978-0-7369-4212-6 (eBook)
1. Wives—Religious life. 2. Husbands—Psychology. 3. Marriage—Religious aspects—Christianity. 4. Man-woman relationships—Religious aspects—Christianity. I. Title.
BV4528.15.M46 2011
248.8'44—dc22

2011008668

All rights reserved. No part of this publication may be reproduced, stored in a retrieval system, or transmitted in any form or by any means—electronic, mechanical, digital, photocopy, recording, or any other—except for brief quotations in printed reviews, without the prior permission of the publisher.

Printed in the United States of America

11 12 13 14 15 16 17 18 / VP-NI / 10 9 8 7 6 5 4 3 2 1

This book is for my husband, Hugh.
You are the reason I've been able to live my dreams.
Now I want to spend the rest of our days
helping you reach yours.

Contents

Embracing the Man in Your Life

D o you have times when you feel as if you walk alone in your marriage? Are there some things you just don't understand about your man that might be driving a wedge between the two of you? Would you like to experience a closer connection, but find yourself uncertain about how you can achieve that?

Well, the good news is that you don't have to feel alone in your marriage anymore. You can be the woman who ministers to your husband in such a way that you draw his heart closer to yours in ways you never imagined you could.

After writing my book *When Women Walk Alone* (now ten years ago), and hearing from many wives who felt alone in their marriages, I started thinking about what we, as wives, could do so that we no longer felt isolated within our marriage relationships. How could we come alongside our husbands and inspire and encourage them and draw their hearts toward us to where they *want* to walk alongside us?

That's when I realized that to walk alone in marriage is somewhat of a choice. I must admit that for a number of years I expected my husband, Hugh, to understand me and therefore to be all I needed and wanted him to be. But in many ways I wasn't putting forth the effort to know a little more about *his* world so I could enter it.

As women, we can read all the books in the world about how to grow closer to God so we can *survive* a marriage. But what about making that marriage really great? What about investing our time in getting to know and serving our husbands simply because we want to love them unconditionally and bring joy into their lives? What about taking ourselves—and all we expect our husbands to be for us—out of the equation so God can work in their lives *through* us?

For years I asked God to change my husband so he can be all I want and need in a man. But eventually I learned that if someone or something I'm asking God to change isn't changing, it's probably because God wants to change *me*. Upon realizing this, I began to spend time with God asking Him to change *my* heart, to help me seek *Him* for the "immeasurably more" that He has for me *and* my marriage. And as I did, He laid it on my heart to quit thinking about *me* and *my* needs—and the benefits of marriage for *my* life—and start discovering my husband's needs and the benefits of our marriage for *him*.

So I asked Hugh—my husband of 23 years—"How can I be a woman who inspires you, who draws you closer, who makes you all you can be?" (Prior to this conversation, my question was usually, "What am I doing that seems to be pushing you away from me?" But that was always too intimidating of a question. My husband didn't want a long, drawn-out conversation that would illicit my defense or tears. He liked the question that was aimed directly at what he needed, not indirectly at what I needed.)

The list he gave me eventually became the table of contents for this book. And after interviewing many more husbands, I realized my husband's list was not unique. He was speaking as a male; and many of the things he mentioned are inherently male. I also noticed that Hugh wasn't asking me to do really difficult stuff. In fact, some of it was even fun. And *all* of it was worthwhile.

When a husband is happy, his wife is happy. When he is treated like a king, respected as a man, admired like a hero, and inspired to be all he can be, his wife reaps the benefits. So you see, this book really *is* about you, in an indirect way. As you come alongside your husband and start living with him the way he wants you to, being for him all he needs you to be, you will end up one fulfilled woman!

Now, you might be thinking, *Cindi, you don't know my husband. How can you say if I start serving him and pleasing him that eventually I'll be happier? And isn't that a little one-sided?*

I've learned that God *is* one-sided when it comes to marriage. He always wants to change the one asking Him for change. He always seems to want to work on the one asking Him to do the work. The starting point for real change in your marriage—real change in your husband—is you. Are you willing to trust God that as you please Him by serving your husband He will make it worth your while? Look at it this way: If you are laying down yourself so you can please someone else (God and your husband), God is not going to make you miserable in return. Trust Him. Trust the process. Get to know your man and love him more. And you'll be glad you did.

This book is about embracing the man in your life by understanding and appreciating him for who he is so that he can be all that he was designed to be for God first, and then for you.

But what if your husband isn't a believer and doesn't have a desire to live for God? Embrace him anyway. And as you do, you will be releasing his heart to discover who he is in God's eyes as he sees first who he is in yours.

Perhaps by this point you're thinking, *Why am I reading another book about what a woman can do for a man? When is it gonna be the other way around? Why isn't my husband reading a book on how to better understand me and meet my needs?* Just in case you're beginning to wonder if the score is even, let me share with you what I believe is God's perspective on the issue.

In Genesis 2:18 we discover that we, as women, were created to be helpers to our husbands. The purpose of our existence is to come alongside our husband and be his partner, suitable for him in every way. That doesn't mean a woman can't know fulfillment in her life without a husband. But for the woman who is married, it does mean God's design for her life is to help *him*.

As you leave more of yourself behind and put more of your husband in front of you, you will find him becoming more of what you wanted in the first place. And you'll find there's more about him to love!

Gary Thomas, the author of *Sacred Marriage* and *Sacred Influence*, says, "You can't make your husband serve you or care for you—but you can focus on helping him, and more times than not, that action alone will prompt him to serve and to care. Even if it doesn't, it will...unleash a great spiritual adventure in your own life."[1]

Are you ready for that great spiritual adventure? This book will help you see the unique heart of your man, how it differs from yours, and how you can use your strengths, softness, and God-given abilities to inspire your man to be all he was designed to be. This is a book on how to better understand your husband so you can help him reach the heights. It's a book on how to be the wind beneath his wings, the inspiration in his song, the light in his day, and the spring in his step. It's also a book on how to draw his heart closer to yours so you will no longer feel you are walking alone in your relationship with him. You'll be walking alongside your man—and loving it.

Now, I realize you may be reading this book because there are changes you'd like to make in your husband. There may be certain adjustments in his attitude or work ethic or spiritual life that you'd love to see. I want to encourage you to begin praying right now, "God, please change *me*." And as God changes you, I trust your husband will change too. You are not the reason he is the way he is. But you have incredible power to encourage, inspire, and support him in a way no one else can. So if you've been praying for a transformation or breakthrough in your husband's life, I want to encourage you to begin praying that the transformation will start with you. Real transformation starts—in our marriages, in our families, in our spiritual lives, and in our personal lives—when we, as wives, are willing to say, "God, start with me."

I'm right there alongside you, sister, praying that as I write this—and you read it—we'll be making changes together, and in the process, helping our husbands be all they can be—for God first, and then for us.

So, are you ready for the changes about to take place? Then take a deep breath...and here we go.

"...if you really want to motivate your man and communicate with him, as well as enjoy a fulfilling marriage with him and raise healthy kids with him, stop expecting him to act or think like a woman. He can't do that. Nor should he."

GARY THOMAS, *SACRED INFLUENCE*

CHAPTER 1

Understanding His World

H ugh walked into the store past the men in suits who were waiting to show him the latest cell phone. "I just want something that I can make calls on," he mumbled to himself under his breath. "No Internet. No texting, no music. Just give me a darn *phone*."

Then his eye caught a rock-like flip phone that he practically had to pry open. "Feel how heavy this is," he said as he picked it up and admired it.

I found myself thinking, *Wouldn't a light phone be better, especially if it's in your pocket?* Hugh continued his admiration of the heavy, durable "man-looking" phone.

Just then a man, soiled from head to toe, came into the store in a rush and out of breath.

"Dude, that is an *awesome* phone," he told Hugh as he saw him holding the model this guy apparently owned.

"I just dropped mine from a height of thirty feet on a construction site and it landed in a puddle of water. The face cracked a little, but it's *still* working!"

That was all it took to sell my husband that phone.

"I'll take this one," Hugh said to one of the suited up men he originally didn't want to address.

I looked at Hugh, wondering what planet he came from. Not only did my husband want a phone that felt like a rock or a heavy tool, and that he had to pry open, but I'm sure he also wanted to go out and drop it 30 feet into a puddle of water just to see how durable it was as well!

"It's a man thing, Mom," my teenage daughter said as she observed the expression on my face.

And she was right.

Men are *not* from Mars. But they *do* act and think differently than women. Certain things make your husband tick that you will never understand. I'm not going to elaborate on the differences between men and women. There are hundreds of books already written on that topic. And you are aware of the differences between your husband and yourself more than anyone else. This book, rather, is about understanding *your* husband's world. And you start doing that by understanding, accepting, and embracing the fact that your husband's world is different from your own simply because he's a man.

I want a light, pretty cell phone, preferably pink and sparkly. My husband wants one with visible screws holding it together and a manly name like The Boulder.

I want it attractive; he wants it functional. I want the prettiest color; he wants the best price. I want to talk it through and really make sure it's the one I want; he wants to buy it and get out of the store.

And that's only the picking-out-a-cell-phone part of our day! Add to that our differences on how we like to spend our evenings, what kinds of movies we prefer, and what our idea of an adventurous weekend would be like, and I'll have enough evidence to present the case to my girlfriends that my husband is *indeed* from a different world than I am.

What Husbands Can Teach Us

My, how we'd like our husbands a lot more if they were more like women. We don't *really* believe that, and we don't actually *want* that, but it's the way we think at times. We want a man who is tender, yet we also expect him to be tough. We want sensitivity, but we also expect strength. We want understanding from him, yet a practical side to balance out our emotions. We want a man who is both male and female at heart. Yet most men don't come that way. And they aren't made to *become* that way.

Yet admit it. You, too, have found yourself thinking…

> *If only he'd be more sensitive.*
> *If only he'd be more interested in what I'm interested in.*
> *If only he wouldn't make such a mess.*
> *If only he'd just listen to me!*
> *If only he weren't so loud!*
> *If only he'd be more romantic.*

If, if, if. What we're really saying is, "If only he were more like… well, *me!*"

My friend, Edie, is a licensed marriage and family therapist. In her first couple years of counseling she saw more than her share of women who were unhappy with their husbands.

"So many women want their husbands to be more like women—to shop with them and go to a chick flick with them," Edie said. But one of the ways a woman can most powerfully influence her husband is to accept that he's a different person than she is and those differences are intended for her growth.

Our husbands' differences are intended for *our* growth?

Exactly.

By coming up against an attitude, behavior, or personality trait we don't like, we are forced to confront our own ability to be loving, patient, understanding, and forgiving. It's our opportunity to practice Philippians 2:3-4:

> Do nothing from selfishness or empty conceit, but with humility of mind regard one another as more important than yourselves; do not merely look out for your own personal interests, but also for the interests of others.[2]

Therefore marriage—that arena in which we are bound to another who is so different from ourselves—is our opportunity to grow. Marriage shows us how selfish we can be, how much more godly we can be when it comes to loving our husbands, and how very much we still struggle with wounds we are expecting our husbands to heal.

I've heard some call marriage a "divine conspiracy"—that God uses the marital union to transform our lives. I believe it, too. I've seen, in my own marriage, God's plan to change both me and Hugh by showing us ways in which we know a little of God's love for one another. And God shows it to me the most when I see ways in which my husband is unlike myself.

But God definitely knew what He was doing when He designed men and women differently.

As a wedding gift to her daughter, Valerie, and son-in law, Walt, author Elisabeth Elliot placed her book *Let Me Be a Woman* into her daughter's hands on her wedding day.

The book, subtitled *Notes on Womanhood for Valerie,* provided instruction on femininity in a marriage—and was written in the mid-1970s as feminism was in full swing. In the early 1980s, when I was 16 years old, my older sister placed that book in my hands and said, "Cindi, you need to read this. It will change your perspective on what it means to be a woman and a wife." My goal at that time was to graduate from college and be an independent career woman in need of no man. I had no desire to marry. I thought a man would simply get in the way of my plans for my life.

Then I read Elisabeth Elliot's book, and it changed my life. Life wasn't about me. It was about serving God. And if He should call me to be a wife, it was about serving my husband too.

It still took quite a few years of marriage for me to realize that life and marriage weren't all about me. They weren't about getting my needs met or finding my personal fulfillment. Rather, they were about dying to self, giving up my preferences for another, learning what it means to truly love. And doing those things, in return, became personally fulfilling as I was obeying God's commands to love.

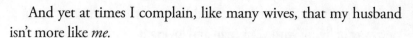

And yet at times I complain, like many wives, that my husband isn't more like *me*.

As Elisabeth Elliot wrote to her newlywed daughter:

> You marry a sinner. There's nobody else to marry. That ought to be obvious enough but when you love a man as you love yours it's easy to forget. You forget it for a while and then when something happens that ought to remind you, you find yourself wondering what's the matter, how could this happen, where did things go wrong? They went wrong back in the Garden of Eden. Settle it once for all, your husband is a son of Adam. Acceptance of him—of all of him—includes acceptance of his being a sinner. He is a fallen creature, in need of the same kind of redemption as the rest of us are in need of, and liable to all the temptations which are "common to man."[3]

There are so many times I forget that my husband is a sinner. Let me rephrase that: There are so many times I forget that I, too, am a sinner. When my husband does something that is inherently male—or just plain human—I sometimes see it as imperfection, as rude, or as unspiritual. It could be all of those things. But it could also be normal.

Elliot goes on to say,

> You marry not only a sinner but a man. You marry a man, not a woman. Strange how easy it seems to be for some women to expect their husbands to be women, to act like women, to do what is expected of women. Instead of that they are men, they act like men, they do what is expected of men and thus they do the unexpected. They surprise their wives by being men and some wives wake up to the awful truth that it was not, in fact, a man that they wanted after all.[4]

Through this book you now have in your hands, I want you to be very glad that you married a man…and *your* man, at that. I want you to begin to celebrate the ways he is different than you and affirm him in areas he never imagined you would. I want you to discover a whole new way of living with your man and loving it.

And if your husband is an unbeliever, or he's just not where you'd like him to be spiritually, I encourage you to stick with me. As you begin to understand his world, become his cheerleader, ease his burdens, make his home a sanctuary, give him breathing room, encourage him to dream, entice him to pursue, and let him lead, you will be allowing him to see how loved he is in your eyes *and* in God's. (I will specifically address a man's spiritual life—or lack of it—in chapter 9.)

I called this chapter "Understanding His World" because there is much to understand and appreciate about it. Yet there's always the woman who says, "But we're in the same world. His world is mine, and mine is his." Yes, to a certain extent. But in a very real way, he is still in a different world than you are. And he always will be. How? He's a man. And therefore, his world—generally speaking—is a bit messier, and he's fine with that. It's louder, and he doesn't notice (women have more sensitive hearing than men). Some parts of his world smell badly and he doesn't seem to notice or care (you have a more keen sense of smell than he does, too, by the way). In his world there are only a few colors (and many more men than women are color blind), but in your world there are ten different shades of red, a myriad of blues, and even lots of different greens. (That's probably why he tends to have only a few pairs of shoes in the closet—a pair of sneakers, a pair of work boots, one set of black dress shoes, and one set of brown casual shoes. You, on the other hand, are likely to have shoes in every color of the spectrum—and that doesn't even cover the sneakers!)

Although studies now show that men and women both speak about 16,000 words per day (debunking the long-lived myth that women outtalk men nearly 2:1), it is also a fact that men and women experience the same level of emotion. What's different is that women tend to be more *expressive* about their emotions than men.[5]

We as women are all about relationships. When you meet another woman and want to get to know her, you will probably ask if she's married, if she has children, and what her children's ages and interests are. By contrast, when your husband shakes hands with another man, he is more inclined to ask what the other man *does*. In a woman's perfect world, she is loved, cherished, and romanced. In a man's perfect world, he is respected. A woman's desires revolve around how she feels. A man's desires revolve around responses to what he does and who he is in the eyes of those around him.

Take a look at this chart for just an overview of how the two of you, generally speaking, differ when it comes to communication, just because you are a woman and he is a man. These findings, by the way, posted on the Internet by Speechmastery, included the following disclaimer: "The list below is general and based on research. Even so, each individual may have qualities that are of their opposite. Some men *will* put the lid down, ask for directions and read the instructions."

Women	Men
Seek out relationships with others	Tend to seek standing and position
Relate to others as equals	Relate to others as rivals
Prefer interdependency, collaboration, coordination and cooperation	Tend toward independence and autonomy
Make decisions based on mutual agreement	Choose or resolve by force, persuasion or majority rule
Desire closeness, togetherness and affinity	Desire space
Care for the approval of peers	Tend to seek the respect of their peers
Express themselves more in private	Express themselves more in public
Are more open to share problems	Keep concerns to themselves
Tend to focus on details of emotions	Tend to focus on the details of fact
More concerned with feelings	Often will not ask for advice, help or directions
May mix personal and business talk	Freely offer advice and analysis
Tend to ask for help, advice and directions	Are problem solvers
Offer sympathy	Tend to look at challenges as a game unless lives are at stake[6]
Display empathy	
Desire to understand problems	
Tend to take a more sober look at challenges	

You may find it helpful to know some of these basic male-female differences when it comes to understanding your man—or at least the components about him that you shouldn't take personally because they are part of his construction, not his attitude!

Incidentally, as I've been writing this book, my husband has enjoyed, on occasion, pointing out to me some of the male tendencies he has that I bristle at, and saying, "That was a man thing. Write *that* in your book!"

His Perfect World

As you begin to understand that your husband's world is a bit different than yours, the question to ask him is, "What would make your world a perfect place?"

This is how my husband answered that question: "A perfect world for me would be working at a job I completely enjoy, having time for rest and relaxation, and knowing that the people closest to me respect, me, honor me, and love me."

There it is—he wants to live from his heart and enjoy what he does, have time to play, and know he is respected and loved for who he is.

But to understand your husband's world isn't just to understand the differences between a man and a woman. (And I know some of you are married to husbands that aren't anything like what we've read about men thus far.) While men share some general traits, every one of them is different. The key is for you to understand *your* husband's world—what makes him tick, what sets him at ease, what he prefers, where he is most "at home," what he avoids, where he shines, and most of all, what makes his heart beat. There will be times when you need to stay out of his world, and times when he invites you to enter it. But don't try to change it. Appreciate it, and your husband will appreciate you even more.

According to the surveys I took of married men of various ages and in various stages of life, I concluded (with my husband's nod of approval, of course) that in every man's world (and most likely your husband's world too):

- He needs to feel respected as a man
- He needs to feel successful in all he does
- He wants to feel like a king, but not be your god

The upcoming chapters in this book will, in many ways, elaborate on these three essentials that are so important to the heart of your man. For now, let's just look at the basics of each one.

He Needs to Feel Respected as a Man

Countless studies have affirmed that a man would rather feel respected than loved. We women long to be cherished and loved and pursued, but there's a sense in which a man can live without love. It's *respect* he can't live without.

It's interesting to note that in the Bible, husbands are commanded to love their wives. And wives are commanded to *respect* their husbands.

That passage of Scripture starts off by telling wives to submit to their husbands, as to the Lord. We would like to think that husbands are commanded first to love us and, as they love us as their own bodies, we will gladly submit. But if we look carefully, we see that in this case, the Bible breaks its usual pattern of laying the responsibility on the husband first. The wives are first commanded to submit to (come under the leadership of) their husbands. And *then* the husbands are commanded to love. This doesn't imply we must earn that love through our obedience. But I believe our obedience and willingness to come under the leadership of our husbands makes it easier for them to obey the tall order God has given them: to love their wives as Christ loved the church and gave Himself up for her.

Here's the passage:

> Wives, be subject to your own husbands, as to the Lord. For the husband is the head of the wife, as Christ also is the head of the church, He Himself being the Savior of the body. But as the church is subject to Christ, so also the wives ought to be to their husbands in everything.

21

> Husbands, love your wives, just as Christ also loved the church and gave Himself up for her…So husbands ought also to love their own wives as their own bodies. He who loves his own wife loves himself…each individual among you also is to love his own wife even as himself, and the wife must see to it that she respects her husband (Ephesians 5:22-25,28,33).

Have you ever thought about why a woman isn't commanded to *love* her husband in return? We are commanded throughout the Bible to love one another, and that includes our husbands. But when it comes to this passage, which speaks specifically about the marriage relationship, God apparently knew a woman desires more than anything else to be loved, and a man desires more than anything else to be respected. God must have known that as we respect our husbands, we are demonstrating love to them in a way they can more easily see and appreciate.

God's perfect design is that as a husband is being respected, he will readily love his wife. And as a wife is being loved, she will readily respect her husband. In a perfect world—which we, unfortunately, don't live in—that would be the case. In our world—which is marred by selfishness and sin, which come more naturally to us than sacrificial love—one of you, you or your husband, must make the first move. Yes, in the second reference of this passage (verse 33), the command is given to your husband first. But the bottom line is that we *both* (husbands *and* wives) are given the command 12 verses earlier in Ephesians 5:21 to "submit to *one another* out of reverence for Christ." Before *any* instruction is given to the wife or husband in that chapter, we see the words "submit to one another." And why? Out of reverence for *Christ*. Show your reverence to the One who gave His all for you by giving your all—your love, your respect, your honor—to your husband. And when you do, see if his love doesn't truly follow!

He Needs to Feel Successful in All He Does

For a man, being productive or successful at something is important. And if your husband isn't, in reality, succeeding at something, he at least needs to *feel* like he's winning. I noticed for a few years after we got married that Hugh would join a game of football without any persuasion. As an all-league wide receiver in high school (having the most yards per reception in the league during his senior year) and one who received letters of interest from several colleges to play ball for them, football was his game. But on one occasion, when my cousins and brother-in-law wanted to play an impromptu game of basketball, it took some persuasion to get Hugh on the court.

"You don't like basketball?" I asked him. He's six feet tall. He's athletic. I couldn't figure it out.

"I'm not very good at basketball," was Hugh's response.

It wasn't that he didn't *like* the sport. He was simply not eager to do something he didn't feel he could *excel* at. Some would call that male ego. Others might call it pride. I saw it as a man thing. A man would rather not enter an arena in which he doesn't feel he can excel. We can learn much from that. A man will gravitate toward the areas of life in which he feels successful. If he is a master at his work, he will spend much time there. If he knows the computer well and can feel successful there, it will occupy much of his time. If he is a whiz with a wrench under the hood of a car, that's where he'll want to be. If gaining knowledge through reading makes him the one who can repeat the facts about any topic of discussion at a party and make him feel more socially comfortable, then he'll keep reading.

Men want to succeed. So what can we, as wives, do with that information? Let your husband know he is succeeding in the areas that are most important to him and you. And if what is important to you isn't necessarily important to him, let him know every now and then that he is succeeding in that area, and it just may become an important area to him after all.

Many a man will give up altogether and go passive when it comes to parenting if you are insisting your parental skills are better. Many a man will stop communicating if you have let him know he is a failure at communication. On the other hand, if you are praising his efforts— even if at this point they are just efforts—he will want to continue to please you. Treat him like a winner at home, and he'll want to be there more often. Praise him for his handiwork around the house, and you'll find him offering to be your handyman. Encourage him and tell him how good he makes you feel in the bedroom, and he'll be more likely to initiate. Encouragement goes a long way…and making your husband feel like a winner will make him want to be around you—especially if you're his No. 1 fan. (We'll look more at this concept in chapter 2.)

He Wants to Feel Like a King, but Not Be Your God

There's a difference between treating your husband with the respect and loyalty you would give a king, and depending on him like he's God.

Many women marry with high expectations, only to be gravely disappointed shortly thereafter when they discover their husband can't possibly meet all of their emotional needs.

Edie, my counselor-friend, sees this a lot in her practice:

"There's a lot of anger on the part of women toward their husbands," she said. "We get focused on our spouse as the one who needs to take care of our needs, and the media adds to that by romanticizing relationships, and we end up projecting our anger onto our husbands for not being the way we expect them to be."

Because your husband is human, he can't possibly meet all your needs. Because he's a man, there are certain ways he will never be able to meet your needs for sensitivity and understanding like another woman. Because he's not your dad, he can't make up for what you might feel was lacking in that relationship. And most importantly, because he's not God, he can't possibly fulfill you in every way.

The quickest way to run your marriage into the ground is to expect your husband to be God in your life—to fill your every need, to know what you're thinking and feeling and be able to respond accordingly, to be your joy, to be your all-in-all. He is a man. He is not able to be all of that for you. He is human, and that means he has weaknesses and will let you down at times. Finally, he is a sinner (as all of us are), and that means he will disappoint you, anger you, and even hurt you more times than he or you would like. So don't look to your husband to be

God in your life, or to fulfill your every need. Instead, look to God as your spiritual husband.

In Isaiah 54:5-6 we read God's words to His covenant people of Israel: "Your Maker is your husband—the LORD Almighty is his name—the Holy One of Israel is your Redeemer; he is called the God of all the earth. The LORD will call you back as if you were a wife deserted and distressed in spirit."

God's Word frequently uses the marriage relationship to illustrate God as our husband. God desires to be a husband to us and have us respond, in return, as we would respond to a husband—to forsake all other gods and love only Him, to respect Him, to dwell intimately with Him, to look to Him for our provision, and so on. There is nothing that will free up your husband to love you more than taking your emotional expectations off of him and leaving them with God. Your husband can then love you in the best way he is able, without feeling he has an impossible task in front of him. (For an in-depth look at this subject, see my book *Letting God Meet Your Emotional Needs*.)[7]

It's pretty simple isn't it? Your husband needs to feel respected. He wants to feel successful. He wants to be treated like a king, but not be your God. His world is simple. Ours is the one that is so often complicated.

✑ From His Perspective ↶

"We're really simple, men are."

Recently, Bill gave his wife Edie—my friend who is the licensed marriage and family therapist—some wise insights into the heart and world of a man.

"We're really simple, men are," he told her.

"I like having a car. I like having sex with my wife. I like good food."

Bill spoke volumes to his wife—and to us about men, in general—with those three sentences.

   1. **He likes having a car.** He wants to be the driver. He likes the feel of being in control of a piece of machinery that can get him from

one place to another. For some men, the nicer or more powerful the car, the better. But ultimately, he just likes having a car.

2. **He enjoys sexual pleasure with his wife.** Men are designed, physically and physiologically, to enjoy sexual pleasure with their wives. Your husband wants to enjoy that activity and experience with *you.* And you are the only one he can enjoy that with and know that he is right and pure before his God. And he *knows* that, even more than you do. (More on this in chapter 7.)

In Ecclesiastes 9:9, Solomon, the wisest man who ever lived, said this: "Enjoy life with your wife, whom you love, all the days of this meaningless life that God has given to you under the sun—all your meaningless days. For this is your lot in life and in your toilsome labor under the sun."

King Solomon wrote a whole book on the meaninglessness of life. And among the few things he found meaningful for a man to enjoy were a good meal and pleasure with his wife. Now think about that! When you prepare a meal for your husband, isn't it your desire that he enjoy it? Similarly, will you prepare yourself for him, physically, as his reward *after* dinner? God paid you quite a compliment when He gave you to your husband as your husband's reward. God considered you a great prize to bring pleasure—in many ways—to your husband. That makes me want to truly be my husband's reward, not his consolation prize.

3. **He loves good food.** And get this…enjoying food, too, is biblical! In Ecclesiastes 2:24, the wise King Solomon says, "There is nothing better for a man than to eat and drink and tell himself that his labor is good. This also I have seen that it is from the hand of God."[8] For a man to be able to sit down and enjoy dinner—or a hearty, messy barbecue lunch!—is one of the ways God rewards him for his work here on earth. So let him eat. It's one of the simple pleasures in life he was designed to enjoy.

What About *Your* Man?

How well do you understand *you*r husband's world? His preferences? His likes and dislikes? The more you understand them, the more you will be able to serve him in his world and make him want to be in no other world than the one you have entered to share with him.

It's easy for a wife to resent the ways her husband is different from her. But I encourage you, dear friend, to celebrate those differences.

Michelle learned to do just that. Her eyes light up when she talks about Leroy, her husband of 17 years. But, she told me, it wasn't *always* that way.

"My husband and I met while very young. We were not walking with the Lord in our youth. In our twenties we headed back to church and got married. It is amazing the grace God has shown on both of us. We haven't had the perfect marriage, but God has brought His wisdom and guidance at crucial times. I have learned my husband's love language, that he doesn't really think about anything at times, that we have different temperaments, and to be his cheerleader. In applying this wisdom to my marriage, I have learned to appreciate my husband. For example, my husband loves to be outside. He is not a homebody. That means we are never home. I have learned to love this about him because I am always experiencing a new adventure. We hike, bike, rollerblade, kayak, travel, eat at different restaurants, and basically sightsee every weekend.

"Now some of you may be wishing this was your husband, but there is a downside to all this. Things do not always get fixed or cleaned at my house. So I think as women we have to learn to accept our husband for who he is. That does not mean you should never address any problems. On the other hand, if you are constantly nagging, you need to think and pray. God may need to change your perspective. During a funeral I attended for a young mother in our Moms group, I was reminded of how short our time can be. Live life with the man you love, not the man you think he *should* be. Life is too short to be unhappy over silly issues. I learned to be happy with the godly man God gave me. My car may not be clean, but I am out enjoying the adventure along the way."

As Robert Jeffress says in his book *Say Goodbye to Regret,* "God gave us a mate to complement us, not to duplicate us (see Genesis 2:22).

Don't try to become like your [husband] and don't expect [him] to morph into a clone of you. It won't happen. And it *shouldn't* happen."[9]

Rather, celebrate his differences. They make him a man; they make him who he is. Keep in mind as well that women tend to outlive men, so there's a good possibility you will one day bury your husband. When you do, all those differences about him will become precious. And you will wish you could have them back again. After your husband is gone, the things that annoy you now—the way he shouts over a football game on the television, or he throws his clothes in a pile in the bedroom (even though you've asked him a billion times to please put them in the dirty clothes hamper)—you will someday look back on and think, *If only I had him around again. I'd be far more patient about all those little things that really weren't such a big deal after all.*

Live without regrets by living well now. Look for those things about him that are different from you and smile. That's what makes him a man. And you are the one he has invited into his male world to share it with him. Love him for letting you in. Live there with appreciation. And know you are more cherished there than you realize.

✆ Entering His Masculine Mind ✆

How well do you know what makes your husband tick?

At an appropriate time (usually after he is well fed or done with dinner at one of his favorite restaurants) ask him the following questions, and listen thoughtfully as he answers. You may discover some precious things about him that you didn't know before.

1. Ask your husband how he relates to the "big three": "I like having a car. I like having sex with my wife. I like food."

2. Now ask your husband what he feels about the essential three:

    - He needs to be respected as a man.
    - He needs to feel successful in what he does.

- He needs to be treated like a king, but not be your god.

Ask him if anything comes to mind with regard to how you can better help him in those three areas.

3. In light of what you have just learned about your husband, write a sentence or two about what you will now do differently in your interactions with him.

☙ A Prayer for You and Your Husband ❧

Lord, Help Me Enter His World...Lovingly

God, You have designed my husband as a unique person and I praise You for that. Help me to see his differences as something to celebrate—that he is uniquely made the way he is to complement and balance who I am. Show me how I can grow and become more loving, more patient, more understanding, and also to be more like You, God, through the differences I notice between him and myself. Help me to walk in his world carefully and responsibly, not trying to change him into someone who is more like me, but appreciating Your handiwork in who he is. Give me the eyes to see unique and wonderful things about my husband that I haven't noticed before, and give me a heart to love him in ways I hadn't thought about. Grant me words, Lord, to express to him, at just the right time, what he means to me. May I learn what it means to love him out of a love and reverence for You, O God.

And as I begin this journey of seeking to understand and affirm my husband in a greater way, give me a steadfast spirit and an enduring heart to see this through, to complete this book faithfully, not giving up if it seems like there's too much to wade through or he's not noticing my efforts. Help me to face each day, each truth, each chapter as a new opportunity to bless his life in ways that I haven't been aware of before. And may You be pleased to draw our hearts closer together along the way.

> "The more encouragement and affirmation he receives from his wife, the easier it will be for him to discern God's voice."
>
> DR. GARY AND BARBARA ROSBERG,
> *6 SECRETS TO A LASTING LOVE*

Chapter 2

Becoming His Cheerleader

Kirk, a 47-year-old businessman, ran into a longtime friend at the airport. He asked his friend about his wife. "Oh, that," Kirk's friend replied. "That was a honeymoon marriage and that was about it. We divorced about a year later. What about you?"

"Alice and I have been happily married 23 years," said Kirk.

"*What?*" his friend replied. "How have you done that? How can *anyone* stay happily married all that time?"

"It's because of my wife," Kirk replied, giving the first answer that came to his mind.

When Kirk returned home from the trip, he told Alice about that short exchange.

"I was floored because I always thought of him as the one holding us together. He's the one who perseveres," Alice said modestly when she recounted to me the airport conversation between her husband and his friend.

When I heard about what had happened, I smiled. What a gift Alice has, that her husband would credit *her* for the reason he's happily married. After hearing the story I picked Alice's brain about her marriage. I wanted to know what it was about her that prompted her husband to give her credit for the success of their marriage. What was it about her that made him adore her so?

As we talked, the answer became obvious. She adored *him*. And it showed.

How can a man not love that? How could her husband not want to be around her? Whether Alice was teaching her exercise class or just talking with friends, she was always his cheerleader.

"I married my best friend," Alice told her exercise class one day. "I got a good one, that's for sure," she said a couple days later. Praise flows off of Alice's lips for her husband of now 24 years. She has learned the fine art of being her husband's cheerleader.

So it's no wonder that Kirk readily credits his Alice (and God) for the success of their marriage. I want my husband to someday credit me (along with God, of course) for why we are still together. Don't you want your husband to say the same about you?

Time for Cheerleading Practice

Your husband lives in a world where it's very important for him to know that he's winning. So what's the best thing you can do for him? Become his cheerleader.

A friend of mine told me that when a man hits midlife he needs his wife to be more like a girlfriend than a mother. I myself think that no matter how old a man is, he wants a cheerleader in his life. (And I'm not talking about a young woman in a short skirt!) He needs a No. 1 fan to cheer him on, support him, encourage him, and believe in him even when he isn't too sure if he believes in himself. And ladies, that No. 1 fan of your husband needs to be *you*.

My friend, Patty, was telling me about a tense moment between her and her husband, Todd. He was about to face his ex-wife over a difficult situation regarding their teenage sons, and Patty wasn't invited to go over to his ex-wife's house with him and be a part of resolving the matter.

"Todd knows I'm mad," she told me. "He was trying to be nice this morning, but I'm still ticked."

I talked with Patty for a while about Todd being in a no-win situation. He had a controlling ex-wife who still wanted a say in her children's lives, and a wife whom he loved but didn't want her to have to be involved in a potentially ugly situation.

"He really can't win with this one," I told Patty. "And he needs your support and confidence in him right now. He might not have said it when he left for work this morning, but more than anything he needs to know you are on his side."

I encouraged Patty to call Todd or send him a text message to reaffirm him and let him know she wasn't angry with him anymore.

She ended up sending a text message: "I believe in you. I know you'll do the right thing tonight. Can't wait to see you when you get home."

The next day when I saw Patty, she was beaming.

"I sent Todd an encouraging text message, and you were right. He was *so* happy. He called to tell me how much it meant to him that I was on his side."

Todd needed a cheerleader in his corner that difficult evening. And his wife came through for him.

As your husband is out on the football field (read: in the boardroom, on the construction site, in the pulpit, at the office), he needs to know you are on the sidelines cheering for him, believing in him, and rooting him on. So what does that look like? How can you, in a practical way, be his cheerleader? By putting into practice the following attitudes and actions until they become habits. And to help you remember them, I've titled them using the acrostic C-H-E-E-R.

C—Come Alongside Him

We read in Genesis 2:18 that after God created the first man, He saw that it was "not good for the man to be alone." So God made a "helper suitable for him."

God made a woman for Adam so he would not have to live in solitude, *and* so he would have the help he needed. She was to be his helper—one who came alongside him and helped him with whatever he needed to do. Author and biblical counselor Elyse Fitzpatrick, in her book *Helper by Design,* says,

> Of course, this help can include physical labor, but that wasn't the main thrust of her design. Remember that Adam had all the purely physical help he needed in the form of the animals in the garden. If he had wanted to move a tree, he didn't need Eve; he had the Behemoth. Also, if the help that God wanted to give Adam was primarily physical, He would have created Eve with more, rather than less, physical strength. No, Eve's helping of Adam was to consist of something beyond mere physical labor, although joyful laboring together with Adam was certainly part of her daily routine.[10]

Eve's role of being Adam's helper is very significant—probably more so than we may realize. In Genesis 2:18, when God said He would make a "helper" suitable for Adam, God used the same word that describes the role and ministry of the Holy Spirit in the New Testament. The Holy Spirit is called our "helper"—and He is also our counselor, comforter, intercessor, and advocate. The Hebrew word translated *helper* in Genesis 2:18 can also be translated as one who brings unique strengths and qualities to the other; these qualities, found only in the woman, complete the union between man and woman.[11] This word is also used in the Old Testament in reference to God Himself in Psalm 54:4, where David tells us that God is our "helper." It is a title of honor and great worth. In giving you to your husband as his "helper," God was giving your man someone who is designed to act, in some ways, as his counselor, comforter, intercessor, and advocate.

Marriage coaches Dr. Gary and Barb Rosberg say, "By understanding the meaning of your role as helper, you can be encouraged to use your distinctive strengths to build up your husband and contribute to his life. Your very uniqueness can offer your husband qualities that fully complete him—as no one else can!"[12] Can you recall times when you just had a feeling about something—or when you exercised spiritual discernment—and you were able to warn your husband about a matter and keep him from a potentially dangerous, tempting, or harmful situation? If so, you have an idea of what it means for you to be his helper—in somewhat the same sense that the Holy Spirit is our helper and the One who counsels, comforts, and convicts us.

One of the best ways you can come alongside your husband and be his helper is to quietly watch and prayerfully wait upon God as you observe your husband's needs and determine how you might best respond to those needs. Just as the Holy Spirit quietly ministers to your heart, you can quietly minister to your husband's heart by being his helper without him even knowing it.

H—Help Him Look Good...Always

Sometimes when my husband and I are conversing with another couple, he will describe something that took place, but in a way that's different than how I remember it. For instance, he might leave out some details, or get some of the little specifics mixed up. And being a former reporter and the self-appointed "keeper and recorder of details" in our marriage, I often feel I have to set things straight. (Alert: What *not* to do!) That must bug the heck out of Hugh.

Is it so important that certain details are recited with perfect precision?

One of my friends, Barbara, says she's often noticed the unattractive pettiness of wives correcting their husbands over nonessential specifics. (Ouch!) "When speaking as a couple to others, if he says the distance is ten miles and it's nine, let it go. Or if something happened on a Wednesday and it was a Thursday, let it go. It doesn't matter. It's not relevant to the story, and your correction of your husband sounds like mothering."

The golden rule comes into play here. Treat others as you want to be treated. Revere your husband in the same way you want to be respected and revered. It will go a long way with him. And that's what a cheerleader would do. "That's okay. That's all right; get in there and fight, fight, fight." (Only not in a motherly, condescending "You can do it, little Ronny" way.)

E—*Encourage Him Personally*

"Letting him know he's succeeding means letting him know he's loved," said Barbara, who works at intentionally showing her husband, Don, that he is loved. Not because he *needs* that, but because she wants to show Christlike love to him. And she knows he, like any man, needs to feel he is winning.

"Once I left a sticky note on his bathroom mirror stating he was an awesome man. Later that week, in a study he was teaching, he mentioned it to the group and he choked back tears. That note flipped a little heart switch—that one sentence, that one comment. I happened to be in the back of the room when he shared about the note, but that wasn't why he mentioned it. It was because of what the note meant to him at the time."

Barbara added, "Never underestimate the unknown guidance of the Holy Spirit for these sweet sound bites or phrases of encouragement. So many times I've done little nothings or made brief comments only to find out that I was prompted to say that for an inner purpose or healing that was needed, which I knew nothing about. I'm able to tell by my husband's reaction—once in a while a tear will well up in his eye, but most typically he gives me a short response that lets me know what I said did far more than what I had intended."

Wow…another example of being a *helper* in the true sense of the word.

Barbara listed for me some ways we can touch our husband's heart through personal words of encouragement: She said she consciously and deliberately makes an effort to say these kinds of things to Don:

- "I desire you, _____ " (insert your husband's name here).

- "You're an awesome man."

- "I'm a lucky gal" (this started because, when we first got married, he would tell me, "I'm a lucky guy").

- "Thank you for loving our family."

- "Thank you for doing what you did for our family."
- "I looked around the room and I gotta tell you that if I had to choose again, it would be you."

Barbara also said that sometimes you can give personal encouragement simply by listening to and affirming your husband, even when you have other things going on that seem more important at the time.

"Sometimes when he's talking and I'm *not* interested in what he's saying, I suck it up, smile, and listen till he finishes what he wanted to tell me. And this could be something like baseball stats, which I am interested in ninety-five percent of the time, but I'm talking about that five percent of the time when you just want to say, 'I'm too busy' or keep looking at your computer or reading a magazine instead of giving him your full attention. During those times, I consciously stop, look up, and listen, all the while giving myself a high-five for respecting and honoring him when I am wanting to do something else. These are the kind of deliberate, self-sacrificing actions that make the difference in letting him know he is appreciated, and that encourages him."

Encouragement from you, his wife, goes further than affirming words from anyone else.

Debbie said she encourages her husband, Marvin, by praising him through e-mails, text messages, phone calls, or face-to-face. "We're in the same workplace, so opportunities abound. The praise is unsolicited and given at thoughtful moments. I make specific comments about things he's done or said, not broad, sweeping statements. He tells me that my comments mean more to him than anyone else's."

Barbara said, "As I was dashing out the door, I hurriedly left Don a note written on scruffy paper torn from a notepad. I left it on the steps of the garage. I wrote, 'Excited about new transitions…start getting fired up…one step closer.' When I asked him what I've done lately that has encouraged or inspired him, he handed me that scruffy note paper. He actually saved it and keeps it in his briefcase!"

Yes, encouragement from his wife often means more to a husband than encouragement from anyone else.

One wife of 23 years told me, "I tell my husband that I respect his hard work, and I try to frequently thank him for it. He has communicated to me several times that it's important for him to hear such comments—especially from *me*."

You can have a profound impact on your husband's life, job, and personal well-being simply by providing a reaffirming voice, a positive smile, a tender touch. As counselor Elyse Fitzpatrick wrote, "I know it's easy to forget, but a wife, because of her nearness, is usually the most powerful human influence in her husband's life."[13]

What kind of influence are you? Do your words tear him down or cut deeply into his soul? I think we've all done that at times, regrettably. But it's never too late to become the kind of wife who builds up her husband and encourages him.

That leads me to the second *E* in C-H-E-E-R:

E—Elevate Him in Front of Others

"A guy wants to feel like he's his wife's hero," Hugh told me.

A few days later, I heard that firsthand from another husband. "Doug" (not his real name) told me he overheard his wife bragging about him after church one morning. Doug does electrical work, and the people who were talking to Doug's wife happened to mention an electrical problem they were having in their home.

Doug said, "There's nothing better than hearing my wife tell someone else, 'My husband is *the* man for that job. He's the *best* there is.' When she says that and really believes it, I'm feeling ten feet tall."

Judy said she lets her husband, Monte, know he's succeeding by acknowledging his accomplishments and his strong work ethic. "I not only tell him, but point it out to our two sons as well."

Scripture gives us a principle for living with one another that is especially beautiful to see in a marriage: "Let no unwholesome word proceed from your mouth, but only such a word as is good for edification according to the *need* of the moment, so that it will give grace to those who hear."[14] That verse implies that other people have a *need* to be built up, and when you think about it, who doesn't? Your husband has that need, too, especially to be built up by *you*. How can we build up our husbands in front of others?

- By not unnecessarily correcting them in front of others.
- By recounting their praises, no matter who is around.
- By showing them respect through our actions as well as our words.

R—*Respond to Him Enthusiastically*

Our body language says much to our husbands, and so do the looks on our faces—the roll of our eyes, the tightening of our lips, an exasperated sigh. How much more would he love to see the light in our eyes, the spring in our step, and the smile on our lips when he comes through the door?

When our daughter, Dana, was three years old, she expressed an uninhibited enthusiasm for Hugh when he came through the door at the end of the day. She would cry out, "D-a-a-a-a-a-ad-d-d-d-d-d-d-y-y-y-y-y-y" and come running to him with her arms open wide. One Sunday, during a sermon, my husband talked of little Dana's response to him when he arrived home, using that as an illustration of what our response might be like one day when we pass on from this life and see our heavenly Father. After the service finished, as people were filing out of the church, I retrieved Dana from the nursery, and when she saw her daddy on the front steps of the church, she cried out and ran toward him. She provided a real-life demonstration of what Hugh had just talked about! Hugh was all smiles as his little girl ran to meet him with arms open wide.

Today, "little Dana" is a five-foot-ten college student. But when she's home on weekends and Dad has discovered it, *he* will come through the door yelling, "D-a-a-a-a-a-n-n-n-n-a-a-a-a-a" with his arms open wide! My, how the roles have reversed.

Then I started thinking, *What if that were* my *reaction each time my husband came through the door?* Instead of him having to yell upstairs to the study (where I'm glued in front of the computer) to let me know he's home, when I hear him come through the door, I should be running down the stairs with arms wide open to welcome him.

Mike, who has been married 11 years and has three young sons, said that kind of welcome makes him feel he's winning too.

"When I come home and my wife greets me with a kiss and the kids come running with arms open wide yelling, 'Daddy' and crashing into me with a big hug, I know I am doing something right," he said. "I feel I am winning in my marriage when my wife feels good about our relationship and how I am meeting her needs."

Rhonda has been married to Steve for 30 years. And she has a way of constantly letting her husband know he's winning by responding to him enthusiastically.

"I think the most important way to encourage my husband in his success is not as much with words as with what is unspoken," Rhonda said. "The smiles, affirming looks, nods, touches, and hugs are priceless. On the other hand, the sighs, groans, or silent treatment when you feel he is not measuring up to your expectations will scream louder than any words of disapproval. If your husband believes you are in his corner, and you are acknowledging his attempts with fond approval, he will attempt to do more than he ever dreamed he could accomplish."

Make Sure *You're* the Cheerleader—Not Someone Else

Kitty, a sweet, soft-spoken kind-of-wife-we-all-want-to-be, shared with me one of the motivating phrases she once heard and has always remembered during her many years of marriage to Dave.

"Dave and I attended a business seminar many years ago. The speaker said something I'll never forget. He said, 'Behind every successful man is a woman—and hopefully that woman is his wife.'

"And I gulped and said to myself, '*I* want to be that woman in Dave's life. *I* want to be the one who makes him feel successful, not someone else.' That encouraged me to treat my husband with respect and to be his cheerleader, not the nagging wife. I don't always understand my husband, but I know I can always be respectful of his ideas and views, and I trust his decisions. He is my hero, and I need to let him know it."

How does she do that?

"I share with others how lucky I am to have such a great husband," Kitty said. "Eventually it gets backs to him."

And one look at Kitty's husband, Dave, is evidence that her years of being his cheerleader has paid off. After nearly 40 years together, Dave's eyes still light up when he talks of Kitty. Several years ago, when Kitty was diagnosed with cancer, anyone will tell you the news was harder on Dave than it was on Kitty. Just the thought she might leave him was unbearable to him. Today, with her cancer five years in remission, she continues to be the spring in his step.

On the other hand, I have heard story after story from women whose husbands found someone else they wanted to be with. And many times, it wasn't about their husband finding a younger, more attractive female. Rather, it came down to the husband finding someone who *admired* him, encouraged him, and thought the world of him. In the long run, those husbands wanted to be with someone who admired them (the cheerleader) rather than around their wives, who had, albeit unintentionally, let the hot embers of their heart's passions for their husbands grow cold through the years.

Now don't misunderstand me. A loss of passion or growing cold through the years is never an excuse for either a husband or wife to exit their marriage or begin an extramarital affair. Hugh and I are aware of cases in which wives had done the absolute best they could to encourage and support their husbands, and yet their husbands *still* went astray. But in our 20-plus years of ministry, we have seen that such wandering is *much less likely* to happen when a wife is a constant cheerleader in her husband's life.

Your husband can, without realizing or intending it, be lured away by a woman who simply thinks more highly of him than you do. So make sure he knows, without a doubt, that *you* are his No. 1 fan.

What Can *You* Do?

Part of my research for this book included interviewing couples who were in some of the strongest marriages I have seen, as well as wives who were strong in their marriages (in terms of holding things together) and were having an impact on their husbands, making them strong, too. Here are some examples of what these committed, persevering, and joyful women had to say about letting their husbands know they are winning:

- "I don't keep score. I respect him."

- "I have always tried to give him verbal compliments and tell him honestly how he's doing and praise his strong points."

- "Sex gives him affirmation and release—it's different physically for men than for women, and it's very important for my husband's self-esteem and his sense of importance and success."

- "I give him words of affirmation. Early in our marriage, I realized that when I pay him a compliment, he wants details! If I say, 'You're such a good dad,' he'll respond, 'How so?' That has taught me to give him specific reasons for why I respect his efforts and actions. I've also learned that it's much easier to compliment him at the time I recognize he is doing something well, rather than letting time go by and trying to remember a compliment to give him later on when I sense he needs affirmation."

- "When my husband completes a chore or project that we've wanted done for a long time, he says he loves it when I praise him for doing it instead of saying, 'Well, you finally got it done.' Praising him encourages him to do more. In his first marriage (his wife left him), he used to get 'beat up' by her for not getting things done sooner."

What do *you* do to make your husband feel like he's winning? How can you be his cheerleader and affirm him as a man? Maybe you're thinking, *My husband is pretty low maintenance. I don't think he feels the need to succeed.* Well, maybe in your husband's case it's more like a need to feel he is moving forward in some way.

ᥱ From His Perspective ᥬ

"It's all about 'forward motion.'"

Steve, a 34-year-old professional animator who has been married 10 years, described what makes him feel like he's winning in life and marriage. And listen closely. It may sound very much like what *your* man feels but doesn't know how to verbalize to you.

"For me it's all about forward motion," Steve said. "If things feel like they are on the right track and continuing to move forward instead of backward or stagnant, it's a win. For me this is the case in all aspects of life. At work, I need to feel like I am achieving something, whether it be pushing the quality of the animation work I am producing, expanding my knowledge and know-how, or impressing the people higher up and causing them to take notice. All are examples of things that would make me feel like I am on the right track for promotion, the expansion of my talent, and gaining value in my field.

"Forward motion in finances can help as well. If it looks like we are saving money and our bank account is growing even just a little bit each month, then we are achieving something. If our bank account is always at the same level or it's stagnant, then it doesn't feel like we are winning.

"It's the same in other aspects of life. Today I cleared the dirt out of the forty-year-old drainage pipes that are supposed to carry water from my house's downspouts to the street. Now that I've cleared them out, my house is less likely to have rainwater destabilize its foundation and cause it to shift. To me this is forward motion in my quest to make the family home more safe and sustainable for years to come. It relieves stress to feel like I am moving forward with my goal to perfect the house we live in. I don't have to worry about heavy rains washing my house away.

"In marriage, forward motion comes in my wife's and my ability to understand each other better and grow our relationship. Recently we had an argument, and right in the middle of it she said, 'I'm not going to argue about this with you,' and walked out of the room. Usually postponing arguments works for us as long as we do indeed get back together to resolve what we've started. But a lot of the times postponing makes me a bit nervous, because if we don't ever get back to resolving the matter, we don't have any forward motion with it. If we are able to get back to the issue, we can work through it and accomplish something by learning more about each other. Even when I realize I've lost an argument to my wife, I can rest at ease knowing that there was still forward motion made by having the argument in the first place and getting to know my wife a tiny bit better in the process."

What About *Your* Man?

Is your husband the kind of man who requires a sense of forward motion? Maybe you're saying, "That's *me*—I'm the type who wants to resolve things after an argument." Many men are task-oriented and driven to accomplish. And to advance, to move forward in some way or another, means to them that they are winning.

Ask your husband what it takes for him to feel like he's winning—at work, at home, with you, with your children. Then prayerfully take before God what your husband has told you and say, "God, change me through this. Make me a woman who can help my husband know, every day of his life, that he is winning in his world."

⋐ Becoming the Cheerleader in His Life ⋑

If you feel you can talk about these things with your husband, again, as I suggested at the end of chapter 1, wait until he's relaxed and in conversation mode. Then ask him the following questions. Remember to listen affirmatively and let him know you value all he is saying, even if it sounds strange to you or you disagree with some of what he says. And keep in mind that your affirmation of who he is and what he says will make him want to open up and talk with you more.

1. In what area of your life do you most need affirmation and support?

2. How can I show you, in a practical way, that I am your No. 1 fan?

3. What do I do or say that tells you I am on your team? How can I get better at this?

✐ A Prayer for You and Your Husband ✑

Lord, Make Me His Cheerleader

Lord, You have made it very clear that You are our greatest ally, that You are our helper, our support, our encouragement, and our strength. Now show me how to make it clear to my husband that I am his strongest supporter on earth, his greatest fan, his closest confidante. Help me, at the times when I don't necessarily agree with what he is doing or saying, to still let him know that I love him for who he is—and that I am on his team, no matter what. Please give me Your heart for him so that I am quick to listen, quick to encourage, quick to extend grace, yet slow to criticize, complain, and correct. Most of all, help me to be my husband's cheerleader, not his mother. When he lays his head on his pillow at the end of each day, may he know, from the bottom of his heart, that he is winning with me and he is winning in his home.

> *"Repeat after me:*
> *'If it's good for him, it's good for us.*
> *A healthy husband is a happier*
> *husband, a more caring*
> *husband, and a more*
> *attentive husband.'"*
>
> GARY THOMAS, *SACRED INFLUENCE*

CHAPTER 3

Easing His Burdens

A shley's text message to me was as abrupt as the news she got. "Rich just got laid off."

"What?" I responded. Then I called her.

"What do you mean Rich got laid off? Doesn't he have seniority there? Isn't he one of their most valuable employees?"

I expected Ashley's reaction to be one of worry and stress. Their oldest son had just started his freshman year at a Christian university that had high tuition fees. Christmas was right around the corner. How would they survive this financially? What would they do? Would she need to increase the number of hours she worked? What would they do about health insurance? Would they have to sell their house?

But none of those concerns were on Ashley's mind.

"He's been there sixteen years," she said quietly. "I just keep thinking about him and what he must be going through right now."

Ashley then explained that her husband had watched many coworkers go through the unnerving layoff process in recent months—packing up the things in their workspace in uncomfortable silence and then being escorted out of the building as their coworkers looked on. She knew how difficult it had been for Rich to see his colleagues go through that. Now he would be experiencing it himself.

Because of the type of work Rich does, security was at an all-time high when one's job was terminated. Ashley was worried about the awkward silence and the difficulty of Rich having to pack up his office belongings and leave the place where he'd been a loyal and valuable employee for most of his married life. "I just want him to be able to get through the next hour," she told me. And her voice cracked as she said, "I just want to get home before he does."

I thought long and hard about Ashley's reaction to her husband's devastating news. She wasn't immediately concerned about all the "What if?" questions that would eventually come her way, I suppose. She knew her husband felt burdened about having been laid off. And instead of adding to his burden with her own fears, she sought to do whatever she could, in that moment, to ease the burden he was feeling.

Ashley did in fact arrive home before Rich that day. And she was able to listen as Rich shared with her how his prayer for the past couple of years had been answered. As he watched many employees leave the company due to layoffs, his prayer had been that if and when his time came, he would be able to leave well—by handling the situation with dignity and being an example of Christlike love to his superiors.

Sure enough, he told Ashley, God was faithful. Rich received the news of his layoff in a cold conference room. Because quite a few employees were released that day, the company was prepared for the possibility of a volatile reaction, the kind that sometimes occurs when an employee of long tenure is dismissed.

After Rich's superiors thanked him for his long years of loyalty and excellent performance, Rich thanked *them* for the opportunity and privilege to be part of the company for 16 years. Standard security measures included being told to not say a word to anyone else, having to pack their office belongings in silence as security stands by, and then being escorted out of the building. As an answer to Ashley's prayer, Rich's response led his superiors to relax some of these security measures, and they allowed him to say good-bye to his coworkers.

"They told me to go ahead and take all the time I needed to say good-bye to my colleagues, shake their hands, and wish them well. They basically let me have some closure and leave well," Rich said.

After Rich told me his story, I mentioned to him that the other blessing in his layoff was his wife: "She wasn't worried about the loss of income or how you'd continue to put your son through college or how you'd make it through Christmas," I said. "All she was concerned about—in that moment she received the news—was you. How you were doing, how you'd get through the day. And how much she hoped to get home before you did so she could be there for you."

Rich smiled and recounted another blessing he had experienced in the midst of being laid off: He had been reminded of what really matters in life. And having a solid marriage with a wife who loved him was one of the things that really mattered.

Later that day I spent some time in self-examination, asking God and myself if I could handle that kind of news from my husband with such grace. Could I think of Hugh before worrying about all the consequences? Could I think of his heart and what he was going through before I started to think about secondary matters? Ashley knew well that jobs—even career jobs—come and go. Money comes and goes. Opportunities and disappointments come and go. But relationships last forever. And hers with her husband was paramount.

Putting Him First

Many women I know have experienced the devastation that comes when a husband loses a job, a job they both thought was secure. And many wise women I've talked to, like Ashley, have recognized the most important priority in such a situation: being a support and encouragement to their husbands in the wake of their job loss.

I have to admit there have been times when Hugh was burdened with serious news and immediately I could only think about the consequences to me and my family. But I can be certain Hugh will have already started thinking about such matters even before I've heard the news. He bears the primary responsibility of providing for his family.

He is already burdened with the what ifs. That last thing I need to do is add weight to his already-heavy load.

As I was writing this chapter, I asked husbands to tell me ways in which their wives could best help ease their burdens. Here is what they said:

- "Be understanding about the everyday stresses in my life."

- "When I need to vent about work or other issues that don't involve you, don't take it personally."

- "Offer or invite me to splurge a little on myself—to go to my favorite place to eat, buy a DVD or CD I've been wanting, or see a movie."

- "Don't try to fix all my problems. Some of them are more complicated than others, and in some cases I might not be in a position to make radical changes. Listen and understand."

- "Have the house in order when I come home. I need to feel *something* is still manageable in life."

- "Try to keep the house peaceful and quiet when I'm home. Sometimes a lot of noise translates to chaos."

- "Be reassuring, ask me how everything is going, and understand the pressures I face."

Mike, who has a high-stress job, works long hours, and has a wife and three young sons to come home to, elaborated on what soothes him most after a rough day:

"There have been many times when my wife greeted me at the door in a sexy negligee, and the smell of perfume and a home-cooked Mediterranean dinner were in the air. We would sit and have dinner for hours. This is a great way to forget the pressures of work and to focus on our marriage and relationship." But, he added, the negligee isn't always so important. Just the peace and calm go a long way: "My wife also does a great job of creating an atmosphere of calm and order out of my world of chaos and demands. Creating a refuge of rest in our home, intimacy in our marriage, and orderliness with our kids eases my burdens."

Throughout this book we'll look at some of the burdens our husbands carry that we sometimes forget about or have little understanding of—burdens like being the one primarily responsible for the provision and protection of their families, as well as the spiritual well-being of their families. So that we don't add further to the many burdens our husbands already carry, here are some principles you can keep in mind so that you are a source of support and encouragement:

Allow Him Time to Decompress

Whether they just got devastating news or are coming through the door at the end of a long day, men—like anyone—need time to decompress. Unlike us, for the most part, they don't immediately seek out a colleague to whom they can vent or talk through their troubles. Rather, they want some time to allow their minds to sort through the variables and process them. By the time they arrive at home, it's likely they may still be processing their difficult day at work, their financial stress, or their disappointment in a friend or colleague. Or they may have just endured an annoying, congested commute. That's the time when they need their space so they can decompress. Or, if your husband has been off work and the roles are reversed and you're the one coming through the door at the end of the day, he still needs transition time for that (more on giving him breathing room in chapter 5).

Rhonda said her husband needs a little longer to decompress than she would prefer. But she has learned to wait it out with him.

"I try very hard to remember that my husband's job requires him to use lots of words throughout the day. When he gets home, I must not take personally that he is not ready to talk about all the events of his day. I have dinner with him and try to observe whether he wants to talk or not. More often than not, our best conversations about his day are in the morning, after he has been refreshed by a good night's sleep."

Through the years, Debbie has learned how to best let her husband of nearly 30 years decompress after a long, hard day.

"I have no expectations of him when he gets home," she said. "When the children were younger, we gave him downtime so he could decompress alone, change his clothes, adjust to being home. Because of his position as a full-time pastor, he has demands on him 24/7. I don't ask for help with the home, or food, or attention. He helps when he can, on his own. I work hard to not ask questions about his day until he seems ready or desirous to talk."

And once he's ready to talk, remember this next one:

Listen—Don't Advise or Critique

It's been said that when a wife shares about a problem with her husband, he will tell her how to fix it, when all she wants is for him to just listen. But when the shoe is on the other foot, we, as wives, often try to fix things too. Or at the least, we'll critique the situation and offer our opinion on how we would've handled it differently. (I'm certainly not proud to say that through the years I've become an "expert" at doing this!)

When your husband is ready to talk, let him—without giving your opinion about what he shares.

Rhonda, whose husband, Steve, takes a while to decompress, can find herself eager to give her opinion when Steve would rather she just take time to listen.

"I need to remind myself not to give advice in an attempt to fix whatever Steve is dealing with," she said. "More often than not, he needs for me to listen while he talks through his thoughts and ideas. And when I do say something, I try to offer suggestions or ask questions rather than 'have all the answers,' which I don't have anyway."

Rhonda added that it's tough to *just* listen—even after 30 years of marriage.

"I am still learning, and I still struggle with wanting to talk while he is talking, or giving him my advice when all he needs is an opportunity to talk. If I jump in, sometimes he shuts down and stops talking—and he never gets back to sharing his thoughts after I've 'taken the ball and run with it.'"

Let Him Know All Is Well in His World

Sometimes in the course of trying to ease our own burdens, we unintentionally lay new burdens on our husbands. For example, sometimes Hugh will say something that rubs me the wrong way. Rather than drop it and give him the benefit of the doubt that he didn't mean for his words to offend me, I begin thinking, *I need to talk this through so it won't bother me.* But when I go ahead and talk it through, I end up placing a new burden on Hugh that tells him all is not well in his relationship with his wife. When I tell him he said something I didn't like, I am inadvertently telling him he has failed at something. Then he feels at a loss over how to fix the problem—and he's not sure how to deal with the situation.

Now, there are times when discussion is healthy for resolving a difficulty between the two of you. But timing is everything. When your husband is feeling burdened, stressed, or tired after a long day of work, that's *not* a good time to start the conversations that are geared to helping make *us* feel better.

Hugh shared with me, in a generic way, some of the things he sees as a pastor when he counsels men. "Many times a man arrives home feeling like he failed at work somehow, and then he finds out from his wife that he has failed *her,* too. Even if he's not doing such a good job of communicating or being what she needs him to be at the moment, she can at least let him know, in some small way, that all is going to be okay in his world."

Sharing the Burden

In Matthew 11:28-30 Jesus said, "Come to Me, all who are weary and heavy-laden, and I will give you rest. Take My yoke upon you and learn from Me, for I am gentle and humble in heart, and you will find rest for your souls. For My yoke is easy and My burden is light" (NASB).

Jesus gave the illustration of a yoke, a tool that is placed upon two oxen who help each other to pull the weight of a heavy load. When Jesus said, "Take My yoke upon you and learn from Me," He was saying, "Get in this yoke *with* Me and we'll *share* that burden you are carrying." Eugene Peterson, in The Message, paraphrases Jesus' words in verse 29 this way: "I won't lay anything heavy or ill-fitting on you. Keep company with me and you'll learn to live freely and lightly."

Jesus' offer to ease the burdens of His people is a beautiful example of what you and I can do, as wives, for our husbands. We can shoulder their burdens *with* them. No, we are not God, so we cannot eliminate the burdens and give the spiritual peace that only God can provide, but we *can* use our God-given ability to be our husband's "helper" and share the load with him in ways that help him live more lightly and freely. Remember what we learned in chapter 2 about Eve being created to serve as Adam's helper? And this role wasn't necessarily for physical labor? Well, whatever the burden, your husband needs his life partner to shoulder some of it with him—whether you do it by offering a listening ear, an understanding touch, or a helping hand that saves him time and energy and lightens his load.

My friend Janet Thompson, an author and speaker, has had the opportunity to serve as her husband's helper in a way she never imagined.

When she and her husband, Dave, married, Janet was looking forward to being taken care of and relieved from the stress of being the sole provider after being a single mom for 17 years. Dave had a great career with all the benefits, and she relished the idea of having two incomes.

But three years into their marriage, Dave was part of a corporation-wide job layoff, and since that time, he has never been able to get work in the field that had been his lifelong career. What's more, he remained unemployed for 18 months, and most recently he was working as a pest control technician. Two months before Dave was laid off from his corporate job, Janet had given up her high-paying career job to go into full-time ministry as an author and speaker.

Janet had prayed that Dave's body would hold up under his labor-intensive job until he could retire. But he needed reconstructive foot surgery and lost his job because of the length of time he needed for recovery.

Yet God has provided. He has blessed Janet with four book contracts since Dave's surgery, so their roles have reversed.

"I was his caregiver until he could get up and around again, and now he has essentially become my assistant so I can have time to write," Janet said. "That took a great deal of adjustment. Dave thought we would spend time together, taking breaks for breakfast and lunch, and I was trying to figure out how I was going to find time to write while he was at home."

They established "house rules" to put boundaries around the time Janet needed for her writing. And now, Janet is able to provide for both of them financially as Dave helps out. Whereas before, Janet helped Dave while he was laid up after surgery.

"Dave said that watching how I took over all the household responsibilities after his surgery—and serve as his caregiver—showed him how much I love and appreciate him," Janet said.

And now, with their roles reversed, Janet has been given the opportunity to not only *help* shoulder a burden, but in some ways carry it herself.

Hopefully for you, helping to ease your husband's burdens hasn't been as drastic a change as what happened to Dave and Janet. But all of us wives have a variety of opportunities to serve as the source of comfort and rest that our husbands need.

Barbara said, "When my man comes home, I don't put on a nightie, hand him a glass of wine along with some cheese and crackers, and lovingly ask, 'How was your day?' At the same time, however, I do *not* jump on him with a list of chores or start in on what I did or didn't do that day. If he asks how my day was, I simply say, 'It was great.'

"No matter what happens, I do not add to his list of things to do."

Here are some other ways that wise wives have helped lighten the load that their husbands carry:

- "I try to create a sanctuary in our home. When he walks through the door, the house is clean, dinner is cooking, and I am there to greet him and ask about his day. I know that sounds a bit old-fashioned, but he likes it."

- "I listen to him and let him talk things out. And I

consciously don't bring up my worries, concerns, or stresses because I have God to go to when my husband needs my full attention and love."

- "I willingly handle all the finances, bills, correspondence, gifts, and laundry so my husband can have some 'free time' when he arrives home. We discuss everything so he always knows where we are financially, and several times in our marriage we have switched these roles. What's important is that he knows I can take over these roles when he needs a break."

- "We pray in bed every night. It's amazing how, when we bring God into our day and night, our requests and dreams, our disagreements and joys, we are drawn closer together and closer to God."

- "If I have the kitchen and house picked up, that helps. Even though he realizes that the presence of two preschoolers makes it a challenge to keep the house organized, he feels more stressed if the house is a wreck. It's okay if the toys aren't put away as long as they aren't scattered all over the floor. It's okay if I haven't paid all the bills we received that day as long as I don't let the mail pile up for three days. He also feels more relaxed if I have a hearty meal ready for him."

- "I usually have dinner cooked and ready for my husband. It may not be the best meal, but I try to always provide some kind of dinner. On some days, I also give him a backrub."

- "My husband's biggest need is to have me available for more than just housework and cooking. I take care of the house management and kids' schedules. That frees him up emotionally to focus on work, which he does from home."

- "I don't expect that he won't want to watch news or sports. He always does, and that is okay with me."

- We spend time talking. I ask him about his day and really listen to him."

- "We take long evening walks together."

- "Some nights he will read God's Word to me, which helps both of us give our burdens to the Lord."

- _____

- _____

- _____

I left three blank lines at the end of the list so that you can record ways that *you* can help your husband by shouldering part of the burden or by making his home a sanctuary. And if you haven't really thought about how you can help, ask your husband. He will help you to know what you are doing—or not doing—to ease his burdens.

⌐ From His Perspective ⌐

"I need support, not a critique."

Dan, an analyst by profession who supervises a couple hundred employees, says that when he is burdened about something, he wants his wife's listening ear, but not necessarily her advice or critique. He needs her support, even if she thinks he didn't handle a situation perfectly.

"Most of the conflicts I have at work involve decisions I've made or things I've done," Dan said. "The *worst* thing my wife can do is play devil's advocate. When I spend my whole day struggling to make the right decision, the most hurtful thing to hear from her is the things that could go wrong with my decision. I know she's trying to help by giving me a different perspective, but sometimes I need support, even if my decision at work was not the best one. I have to live with the bad decisions I make, and I can't go back in time. One way my wife can help is to listen and try to understand my perspective first, rather than play devil's advocate too quickly.

"On the other hand," Dan said, "the very best way my wife helps me is when she listens to my problems, then reminds me of God's ability to care for me. She will say, 'Okay, let's make a list of what we want to pray for.' That is *immensely* helpful."

Bob, a 59-year-old husband who is currently out of work, shared his thoughts on the subject of shouldering a difficult burden.

"Sometimes the burdens I carry are completely illogical. And my wife could say 'Really? That's stupid to be concerned about that.' But the way she understands and supports me when I talk about my burdens is a way she helps lift them from me. She will sometimes explain to me that my burdens aren't real or I shouldn't be concerned about them and then she'll explain why—not in a lecturing way, but in a way that provides comfort, by reminding me that God is able to work in and through the situation."

Now's *Your* Chance

Do you have a husband who just needs to vent sometimes? When he does, find out what he needs the most: a listening ear? An understanding look? An affirming touch? Knowing what speaks comfort and understanding to him will help you meet him where he is and be a helper who not only comes alongside him, but who lightens his load as well.

✑ Comforting His Heart ✑

Now it's time for you to ask your husband how you can best ease his burdens. The most important thing for you to know is what ministers to *his* heart when he's tired, disappointed, stressed, or discouraged. Find a time when he's relaxed and ask him:

1. What is the one thing you need from me the most when you come home after a long day?

2. What are some ways I can help you, throughout the day, so you're less likely to feel stressed, tired, or discouraged?

3. On a scale of 1 to 5 (1 being most important and 5 being least important), rank the following in terms of what you need most when you want to talk things out or just vent your feelings:

>   Encouraging words
>
>   Affirming touch
>
>   Quiet attentiveness and understanding
>
>   A smile and the verbal reassurance that you are loved
>
>   Helpful advice
>
>   Other: _____

(And ladies, if his answer *is* sex, well…that chapter is coming!)

ᥱ A Prayer for You and Your Husband ᥲ

Help Me to Be a Burden Lifter

O God, I know You care about my husband, and that You, more than anyone else, understand the burdens he carries. Thank You for being One who offers to help carry those burdens for him so he can live freely and lightly. Help me to be like You, Lord Jesus, by offering to shoulder the load my husband carries so he will not feel alone in the stress or tension he faces day in and day out. Grant me the wisdom to know how to ease his stress and lighten his load at the end of a long day. I truly want to be his helper in every sense of the word. Give me discernment to see when he needs a listening ear, a comforting word, or a reaffirming touch. And may my smile, my words, or just my presence represent relief and peace to him. On days when he doesn't feel he can verbally express how he's feeling, help me to be patient until he's ready to talk. And when he is ready, help me to be quick to hear and slow to speak, so that he can safely lay his burden down at my feet—and Yours.

"It is better to live alone in the corner of an attic than with a quarrelsome wife in a lovely home."

PROVERBS 21:9 NLT

"O Lord, in all generations you have been our home."

PSALM 90:1 CEV

CHAPTER 4

Making His Home a Sanctuary

When I began asking men to tell me what primary way their wives could help ease their burdens, I must admit I expected them to start talking about sex. But they didn't. I then thought they would mention backrubs, foot massages, or dinners out.

But their answers came as a surprise to me. Nearly all of the men interviewed for this book—representing a vast range of ages and years married—indicated that one of the best ways their wives could ease their burdens is to take care of their home.

Not a backrub? Not a dinner out? No. *Just take care of things at home.*

So I've devoted an entire chapter to the subject of making his home a sanctuary.

Now lest you think that's archaic or stereotypical or even sexist, let me shed some light on this matter.

I don't consider myself a real "home" person. I'm not very good at decorating, and our busy schedules don't allow me to cook for the two of us often. But even *my* husband (who loves to eat out and isn't picky about what his house looks like) said, "The best way you can eliminate some of my burdens is to take care of the things at home that I can't, because I'm working. Keep the house clean. Keep up with the laundry. Keep track of the activity calendar. I need to know someone is managing things on the home front."

And that isn't just my husband, ladies. Listen to what other husbands say:

Ken, a lawyer, seeks—and is able to find—solace at the end of his workday, at home: "My wife eases my burdens at the end of the day by doing a good job of keeping on top of things at home. She plans the meals and often will have dinner ready when I get home. She's been the one to balance the bank account and keep track of our spending. Sometimes our girls will get into arguments, or one of them won't live up to their responsibilities. Mary works to get these issues handled without having to bring them to Dad."

Dan, who has a high-stress government job, said his burdens are eased and he feels most relaxed when he has a neat, clean area of his home in which to rest: "A clean room in which I can relax is what I need the most, because clean means there's nothing for me to *do*. If I see clutter or dirty dishes, I can't relax. The less there is to do, the better. I'm seeing more than ever that taking vacations *away* from home is very important because it's the only way I can relax. The only places where I can relax at home are a clean living room and in the bathtub!"

And Steve, a young professional in his thirties who works around technology all day long, said, "I get stressed out easily from work and other things, so I need my home calm and filled with fresh air, sunlight, and plants. At night, I like lit candles and music (satellite radio, which doesn't have all the annoying commercials). Also, we spend ninety percent of our lives on a computer or in front of a TV, so for me, at home, I like rooms that appear to be technology-free. We love having doors on our TV cabinet so we can hide the set from view. Most people let technology have a prominent place in their house. They have oversized TVs that dominate a whole room. We prefer to have the TV hidden when we have friends over. That helps makes things more calm, makes me less stressed, and reminds us of what is important."

The Importance of His Home

Because our husbands are constantly faced with the burden of providing for and protecting their families, anything we as wives can do on the home front to assist them is usually seen by our husbands as a gesture of love and respect.

In the Bible, the most-quoted description of a truly good wife is found in Proverbs 31:10-31. Every verse in that passage refers to a wife's role as her husband's helper, and many of them specifically refer to her help in the affairs of his home:

> A truly good wife is the most precious treasure a
> man can find!
> Her husband depends on her, and she never lets
> him down.
> She is good to him every day of her life, and with
> her own hands she gladly makes clothes.
> She is like a sailing ship that brings food from across
> the sea.
> She gets up before daylight to prepare food for her
> family and for her servants.
> She knows how to buy land and how to plant a
> vineyard, and she always works hard.
> She knows when to buy or sell, and she stays busy
> until late at night.
> She spins her own cloth, and she helps the poor and
> the needy.
> Her family has warm clothing, and so she doesn't
> worry when it snows.
> She does her own sewing, and everything she wears
> is beautiful...
> She is strong and graceful, as well as cheerful about
> the future.
> Her words are sensible, and her advice is thoughtful.
> She takes good care of her family and is never lazy
> (Proverbs 31:10-22,25-27 CEV).

And what is her family's reaction to all she does?

> Her children praise her, and with great pride her husband says, "There are many good women, but you are the best!" (verses 28-29 CEV).

Why is taking care of his home and family so important to a man? Why would it cause him to say "Many women have done wonderful things, but you've outclassed them all!"?[15] Why is it even more important, at times, than a personal touch? (Note that there are no references to backrubs or foot massages in that portion of Scripture!)

It's because home is a man's refuge. It's his safe house. It's the place where he can be himself.

A man's home is also a reflection of who he is. Now, we women like to think of our homes as a reflection of us. And many of us have decorated our homes so they reflect our preferences and personalities. Many of us have been given permission, by our husbands, to do what we want to make home a nice place. Or perhaps you've taken that initiative on your own.

Whatever the case, the place that houses your husband and his family is a reflection of what he's worked for and what is important to him. In that sense, your home is his sanctuary.

His Home, His Refuge

"A man wants his home to be several things," Hugh told me. "A castle where he feels like the king who provides protection and security for his family; a showroom where he can display the fruits of his labors [I know you're cringing as you're thinking, *Oh no...deer antlers on the walls!*]; and a sanctuary to where he can retreat at the end of the day or week and find solace, peace, and a break from the world."

You can ease your husband's burdens by seeing to it that his home offers these things.

A Castle for Your King

A king leads. A king is respected. All bow and rise when he walks through the door. Okay, it probably won't look like that when your husband comes home, but when he steps in and no one acknowledges him, how does that make him feel? True, there might be times he wants to slip in the door and go to a quiet room in the house. But he still wants to know his family is glad he's home.

A Showroom for His Labors

We don't have antlers on the walls of our home. Now, if my husband ever shot an elk, it might be a different story. But my husband does love to travel and experience life. When we got married we talked of storing up memories and experiences, not things. And so in our home, we have many family pictures of our travels and relics that serve as reminders of our visits to other countries. In fact, we have one tiny downstairs bathroom that Hugh suggested we take the "country clutter" out of so he could decorate it the way he wanted. *What on earth is my husband going to do in that bathroom?* I thought.

Well, Hugh placed spears from Papua New Guinea on either side of the toilet, hung a couple of African tribal masks on the wall behind the toilet, draped an Egyptian print fabric over the mirror, and placed a woven rug and wastebasket on the floor. He even picked out some hand towels for the towel rack that matched the color scheme of his artifacts and there it was—the "Wild Man" bathroom, we call it. He's very proud of that one little bathroom in our home. It's the one room he decorated completely on his own, and it reflects much about who he is and where he's been.

A Sanctuary Where He Can Rest

One of my friends was recounting to me the difficulties her husband was experiencing through his leadership role at work and at church. "His home is the only place left that feels safe," she said. I had never thought about that before, nor would I expect to ever hear a man put it quite that way. But for his sake, his home *must* be safe. It needs to be a place where he isn't going to be criticized or scrutinized (like he might be at work), where he doesn't have to impress others (like in the boardroom), where he knows he is loved and all is okay. It should also be the place where he can relax and have some peace and quiet. If you have young ones running around, have a "quiet zone" where your husband can go when he needs time alone, or adopt a "No kids in Daddy's study" policy. And teach the kids not to scream or argue in the room next to where their father is resting.

Mike said, "I need an area, a retreat I can go to, a space I can maintain however I want. Essentially I want a man cave for reflection, tinkering, and where no one can disturb my peace and tell me about the next 'thing' that has to be done or fixed. In our house, this place is the garage workbench!"

It's important that a man doesn't feel patronized by only being offered some remote corner of the house where he has permission to do whatever he wants (you know, the garage, his den, or the area around the barbecue). A better approach is to partner with him on the feel and look of the whole house. Some men would like to have the opportunity to give input on what their homes look and feel like. Others, however, are simply interested in having a place of their own, a place where they can be themselves.

When He Longs for a "Cave"

My friend, Edie (the counselor and therapist I quoted in chapter 1), found a way to give her husband a "man cave" that many husbands often dream about. She said it came about one day in her home after her son told her, "Mom, have you noticed you've taken over every room in the house?" She hadn't noticed. But she realized then that her husband, Bill, needed a place of his own.

She had just moved her office back home and decided to switch rooms with Bill and give him her upstairs study so she could use the downstairs bedroom for her office. Edie realized this was Bill's opportunity to do his own thing with one of the rooms in the house. "He painted the upstairs room green and we call it the 'man cave,'" Edie said. "Just calling it the 'man cave' gives him approval to go there." So if Bill is grumpy, all Edie has to say is "Would you like to go to your man cave?" and that is Bill's permission to withdraw and have some time to himself.

"He wanted a TV in his man cave, too, so he could go there and just veg out. It has to be his things, organized his way, so I can't be moving knickknacks around and all that in my effort to keep it neat-looking. Plus, his room is upstairs, so no one has to see it!" she said, laughing.

Bill's desire to have a man cave made Edie realize that it's *his* home, too, and he has been the one working and paying for it, so he really should have more say in how it looks. She recently asked Bill, "If you could change anything about the house—décor wise—what would it be?" He pointed to two high "open areas" built into the wall (near the ceiling) that were empty. Edie liked them empty. But Bill said, "I'd like to see something in those open areas." So Edie climbed a ladder and placed an artificial plant in one open area and a large trunk and a clock in the other.

Giving Him Some Space

Theresa realized her husband needed some part of the home for his own personal space as well. "My husband created a music area in our bedroom where we have a little nook or alcove," she said. "He has all his musical instruments and equipment there, and it makes the room look cluttered, but I refuse to complain about that. There isn't another room available to serve as a music room right now. He and our son have also taken over the garage with their surfboards and such, and I don't complain too often about their equipment and the sand all over the house. My husband has to have places in the home for *his* stuff too."

Lynn said her husband needs not a section of the home, but a clean and tidy home.

"My husband needs a calm, clean, and uncluttered home," Lynn told me. "He enjoys that I decorate a little for each season and holiday. He loves his 'cave' (there's that word again!) and it gives him peace to have free time to read in his recliner—and to read whatever he chooses."

One wise wife said she makes her home her husband's sanctuary simply by being there for him.

"I schedule time with friends at the same time that my husband is out, so that we're not out of the house on different nights. If he's home,

I try to stay home. My husband is my ministry. I'm here for him even if he's studying, writing, or watching an Angels baseball game all at the same time and I'm upstairs. I'm still here for him. And occasionally I'll surprise him with cheese and crackers or a piece of pie to help break up the time. The way to a man's heart is still through his stomach. If he likes hot dogs and you think they are disgusting, surprise him with a hot dog over a baseball game."

Here are some other things wives have done to help make their homes a sanctuary for their husbands:

- "I try to keep the kids from hounding him as soon as he walks through the door."

- "I try to have a peaceful house when my husband gets home. I make an effort to keep the house neat and not chaotic, although having two teenagers in the house makes that a real challenge."

- "I keep the house a sanctuary for him by not planning a bunch of things too closely together and letting it become like a circus. Too much activity in the house drives him crazy."

- "I don't do chick talk on the phone in front of him. I go in another room so he doesn't need to be subjected to the drone of it."

- "Our bedroom has been redecorated as our special place. We have candles, a sitting nook, a soft rug for bare toes and long conversations, and pictures of us as a couple. It's always clean, and never a catch-all."

So that's what some wives do to make their homes a sanctuary for their husbands. And what do their husbands think? Without knowing how their wives responded, this is what they had to say about making their home a sanctuary and a desirable place to be:

- "Keep the house neat and clean; don't let it become a big mess."

- "Let the décor and furnishings also reflect his likes."

- "Always ask him first when you want to invite people over or plan a social at the house."

- "Keep the noise to a minimum. I enjoy the peace and quiet of a home."

- "Peace, support, kind and gentle words, smiles, warm touches. Love and peace are what I need most."

So you see? It isn't about doing an expensive remodeling project in the house. And it's not about putting elk antlers on your living room wall. It's about creating a safe, quiet, nurturing place so the king can rest after a long day of work. It's about putting your love for him into action by creating a warm, inviting home in which he can seek refuge and rest.

First John 3:18 says "Let's not just talk about love; let's practice real love."[16] And you can practice it by making your home a place where your husband longs to be.

ⅇ⁓ From His Perspective ⁓ᑫ

"A man's home *is* his world."

Bob, a 59-year-old husband and father who has been married 35 years, said that a man's home, his sanctuary, is basically his world.

"A man's home is pretty much his world. Men can act tough and say that their job or work is their world, but if you narrow it down, it's really his home that is his world. If work is not going well, he can always get another job, or do something else, or take some time off. But if his home is messed up, he's shot.

"Any problem in the home will just follow him around wherever he goes. That's why men who leave their marriages to get out of a problem create new ones in whatever relationship they enter. That's the reason we see some people who have gone through two or three divorces. They are the problem, and they keep taking the problem somewhere else.

"My home is pretty much my world. I want it simple. I want it uncomplicated. I want things in order. There's organization to the home and the relationship. When all is going well in my home, I feel a sense of contentment. And when there's contentment at home, it has a way of spreading out to other areas of my life. If I'm content at home, I'm content at work. If I'm content at home, I'm playing better golf. If I'm content at home, I'm a happy man.

"I think of my home as a sanctuary. Just like you go into a 'sanctuary' to meet with God and experience His unconditional love, grace, and forgiveness, so I want to experience those things in my home as well. I need my home to be a place of love, understanding, forgiveness, peace, warmth. In that way a man's home—my home—is a refuge, because in it you get what you don't find outside in the world."

ℰ Creating His Sanctuary ℐ

All right—here is where I'm asking you, as a wife who wants to inspire your husband, to be daring and ask your husband if there's anything he'd like to change in the home you two share: the décor, the colors, the furniture, having a "man cave" (come on, you know you need to at least *offer*). Listen with an open mind to his suggestions, and if you sense there is something missing that would mean a lot to him or something you can do to help make your home more of a sanctuary, prayerfully ask God how you can begin to make it happen. (Some things really *are* possible; we just haven't asked God for them or talked to someone who can help us make it happen.)

Once your husband gives you input, begin your project—with his guidance of course. If he's the kind of man who simply doesn't care what your house looks like, ask him about the nonmaterial things: What kind of mood do you look forward to when you come through the door? Are there certain smells or fragrances you prefer? (Some men just *hate* those expensive aromatic candles we women seem to love and would prefer the smell of good food in the oven when they enter the door. (In which case a vanilla- or pumpkin-scented candle might do the trick!)

Finally, talk with your husband about what he needs in his home by asking him the following questions:

1. How would you describe your home?

   a. a castle for his highness

   b. a combat zone

   c. a sanctuary of peace

   d. other: _____

2. What kind of home atmosphere and mood do you prefer most?

3. How can I make our home feel more like a castle where you are the king?

4. Is there anything you would like to display that represents the fruits of your labors? (Be open-minded on this one. Again, giving him one room or a section of a room could be a workable solution.)

5. Would you be interested in a "man cave"? (You may want to read to him the description of Bill's man cave. Don't be scared, just ask. He might surprise you with his answer.)

6. Do you have some suggestions for how I might incorporate your preferences into our home or future home? (Make sure you listen to *his* ideas instead of offering—or insisting upon—your own ideas here.)

A Prayer for Your Husband and Home

Create in My Home a Sanctuary, Lord

Using David's prayer of repentance in Psalm 51 as inspiration—where he asked God for a new heart, clean and restored—I've developed a prayer each of us can lift up when we offer our homes to God to be remade in a way that ministers to the hearts of our husbands, and is therefore an offering from us to our Lord.

Have mercy on our home, O Lord, according to Your great love. In Your compassion blot out every bad memory that has ever occurred here and everything that has made our home a stressful place rather than a peaceful sanctuary for this family.

Sweep out the stress, blow out the tension, and pour into this home Your cleansing power and comforting peace. May our home be a reflection of our hearts—clean, well-kept, joyful, and bearing nothing we would be ashamed for the outside world to see.

Let laughter ring through the hallways as we who have regenerated hearts live in the light of Your love. Create in each of us pure hearts that seek You, even if it starts with me. Teach us to be grateful for all You've given us and to be aware of what truly matters within the walls of this home.

Restore to us the joy of being together and being in Your presence, and give us a spirit that is willing to endure whatever comes our way as a family. When we are together here, under this roof, may we be ever reminded we are a loyal team that looks after one another and loves each other unconditionally.

You are welcome here, Lord Jesus. Make our hearts Your home…and make our home a reflection of Your heart.

> *"Because you've always
> stood up for me, I'm
> free to run and play."*
>
> PSALM 63:7 MSG

CHAPTER 5

Giving Him Breathing Room

I learned early on in my marriage that even though my husband loved me, he didn't have the need—nor the desire—to spend *every* waking moment with me. And the times he has needed his space have been more about him needing space from *other* things, and not me.

Men often desire space (or "veg time," as Hugh calls it) to escape the pressures of work, to get a little exercise if they've been holed up in an office too long, to process something that is weighing heavily on them mentally, or to get outdoors and breathe some fresh air.

"I need a few minutes each evening to have some calm and quiet," my brother Dan told me. Dan has been married nearly 20 years, has a stressful government job, and has two children in middle school. "My wife can be right there with me—it's not *her* I need the break from. I just need to mentally escape the pressures of my job. I can escape into the bathtub, but can just as easily sit with my wife on the couch and read or watch TV or do something that doesn't require much thought or action."

It's when we push our husbands to talk, or ask them to share their day with us, or we give them a "to do" list that they may end up desiring some space from *us*.

I asked other husbands to tell me what their wives can do (or what they'd *love* for their wives to do) when it comes to giving them space or helping them decompress when they're feeling like they need space.

"My wife can help me most by learning to sense when I'm stressed and knowing I need those times to just unwind," Hank said. "I want her to understand that my 'veg time' doesn't mean I don't like being around her or anyone else. It just means I need time for a bit of solitude."

Mike said, "If my wife can wait until at least thirty minutes after I have returned from work to tell me about the next project or item that needs my attention, that would really help provide me with the space I need."

Scott said, "If helping me to relax or get recharged means taking a short trip with friends or doing something solo, like an overnight hike, I'd like her to encourage me to do it."

And Rich said his wife can encourage him to take some time for himself. "If I'm not given permission to take a few moments for myself, I tend not to do it."

Giving Them the Okay

Men are naturally wired to be doers, fixers, and hard workers. And they will push themselves into the ground if their wives let them. A wise wife realizes it's important, healthy, and at times healing for her husband to have some breathing room—some space or downtime that allows him to just be himself.

Jini has been married to Paul, the pastor of a large church, for more than 25 years. And she said she has learned by now that he needs to have time for certain recreational activities to feel like he has his space. And how does she give him that space?

"He gets to golf whenever he can," she said. "I've stopped expecting him to 'get over it.' It is *his* thing."

Michelle said that by giving her husband, Leroy, space in an area that he desired, she eventually got to be a small part of it, and now it's something they enjoy doing together.

"My husband loves to cycle. It is his outlet for stress. I give him time after work and on the weekends. I never put any restraints on him about being home for dinner at a certain time. It creates a little work for me to serve his dinner late, but it is worth it. If your husband has a healthy outlet, it is good for both of you. Recently, while training for a triathlon, Leroy started having me ride with him one day a weekend. Now I get to enjoy one day with him in his hobby that was originally something he did by himself."

And Judy said, "I try to give Monte space by not making our 'to do' list too long or urgent. That way, he can relax on a weekend if he wants to."

For some men, having breathing room is as simple as being allowed to watch TV—or simply *do nothing*—without feeling guilty.

"Another way I try to give Monte space is by encouraging him to watch TV or unwind on the computer without feeling guilty," Judy added.

Janet added, "My husband said I allow him to 'veg out' when he needs to by not complaining when he watches golf on TV or by letting him watch old James Bond movies."

Space Helps Him Accomplish and Re-energize

Theresa has wisely recognized that her middle-aged husband needs space to pursue some of the things that are on his heart.

"My husband loves to write his own songs, and I give him as much space to do that as possible. I try not to ask him to pick up the kids, or stop at the store or some other place after work, so that he can just come home and do whatever he wants to do.

"The main goal I have for my marriage right now is to give my husband the space he needs to unwind or think or do whatever. There's no complaining or guilt trips from me, unless I really need his help with something, such as helping the kids with their homework."

He Said, She Said

Ken said Mary, his wife of 22 years, understands well the concept of giving him the space he needs. And it works well in their home because of their differing schedules. In many marriages, one spouse is a night owl and the other is an early bird. Well, Ken and Mary will both confirm that such a combination has its advantages when it comes to finding time for solitude and breathing room.

Ken said, "Mary and I are usually on different sleep schedules. She goes to bed early; I'm up until about eleven at night. She understands this is my wind-down time and tries to avoid loading it up with tasks. Also if there are things I want to do, as long as they don't interfere with family priorities, then it's okay for me to do them. If Mary feels like I'm working too much or have taken on too much at church, though, she'll speak right up."

Mary said, "I encourage Ken to go on men's retreats and to stay in touch with his brothers and have male friendships. What Ken really loves, though, is reading in the evenings. He has his routine of reading for a few hours each evening, and I don't interrupt that time or ever ask him to give it up. I enjoy seeing him relaxing and reading on the couch, and he makes this alone time late enough that it does not interfere with family time. It helps that I am early to bed and he stays up late."

Loosening the Grip

Sometimes it's easy to take it personally when our husbands want some space from us. But when we see this as a natural part of being a man, and not an insult or injury, it helps us to allow them to take that time without feeling guilty. In Scripture we read several instances of Jesus withdrawing from His closest friends for a time of solitude. On one occasion when He left, others didn't understand. "People are looking for You," they complained. (In other words, "Jesus, You're a big hit right now. Everyone wants to be around You. Why are You disappearing like that?") Scripture says in some cases Jesus withdrew to pray. But in other cases, all we're told is that He "withdrew." We can spiritualize that and say we all need time away to be with God, which is absolutely true. But we can also see that withdrawing as evidence of Jesus' humanity. Like any person, Jesus needed to decompress. He needed some quiet and solitude when the crowds got bigger and the work got longer and the needs became more demanding.

Realize also that such alone times can be spiritually beneficial for more than just prayer. Time alone somewhere—out in the woods, on the beach, up in the mountains, or just sitting in a lawn chair in the backyard—can help your husband to reconnect with God or have some much-needed time to process his life, figure out a problem, or recharge his batteries.

If Jesus, being fully God *and* fully man needed His times of solitude, you can bet your husband needs them too, maybe even more. He also needs space to have time with friends.

So can you give your husband the space he craves? It's not difficult, really. It's more a matter of being aware of the things that exhaust him and, in some cases, make him want to *run*. Here is some advice I've learned from women who have been married for 25, 30, or more years. So yes, they should know.

Spare Him the Chick Chat

Barbara, a pastor's wife and a mentor to many young wives, said she gives her husband space by not expecting him to be one of her girlfriends.

"I don't do the wife thing like talking girl stuff, rambling, or going on and on about topics that truly would be inane to him," Barbara said. "One of my discipleship tips to women is 'Don't fret that your husband doesn't talk or listen or "go deep" with your feelings. That is what girlfriends are for.' Men are not wired for that, and the biggest mistake women make is interpreting this to mean their husbands don't care. Well, they don't, but that doesn't mean they don't care about *you*. It means that girl chat and gossip and those rambling topics bore him to death. Yes, as his helper, we listen to *his* inane topics, but it isn't reciprocal."

Spare Him the Smothering

Men who never get a chance to do anything without their wives can tend to feel smothered. Even if you're taking care not to smother your husband, it's a good idea to give him some breathing room—even if he doesn't realize he needs it. Insist that your husband go out and do things with his friends once in awhile.

One California friend said, "When I heard about a men's retreat in Virginia, I told my husband he needed to spend time with his brother and nephew and just get out of town. He was hesitant at first, but thrilled that I wanted it for him."

Rhonda said Steve's social interaction with other men is essential for him, even though he's a pastor and is around people often.

"I try to support Steve getting together with other men who encourage him—especially men who make him laugh," she said. "I try very hard not to make him feel like he has to wrestle with me to get some time alone or with his male friends."

Lisa, who has been married to Rick for 25 years, said she encourages him to take an occasional weekend trip, go to a concert, or attend a game with the guys.

"I'm not threatened by nor do I have a need to control that area of his life," Lisa said. "He needs to have outside interests. So I often tell him, 'Go play.'"

Jodi's husband works 12-hour workdays during the week and therefore feels guilty being away from their two young sons on the weekends. So he tries to schedule time with his buddies while their sons are napping, if possible.

"Yet I noticed he really does need some guy time so he doesn't go stir-crazy," Jodi said. "It's better for him to be gone a few hours on the weekend and be in pleasant spirits the rest of the time with us, compared to spending 100 percent of the weekend with us but being edgy. If you keep your man at home all the time, he's going to feel smothered. So encourage him to take a bit of time to be with his male friends."

Spare Him the Hovering

One of the things that used to bug Hugh early on in our marriage—and would bug him today if I were to try it again!—is hovering. If I'm reading something over his shoulder, staying in the room to listen to how he handles a phone conversation or a situation with our daughter, or simply checking up on him to see if he did something I asked him to do (or to see what it is he's doing at all!), it sets him on edge. "It's a space thing," he told me. "And it's a trust thing," he later told me. "Don't feel the need to check up on me. Trust, instead, that I'm managing myself and other things wisely."

When our daughter was in elementary school, we had a couple of her friends come over to swim one day. One little girl came with her younger sister, accompanied by their dad. Dad sat and talked with Hugh as the girls swam, one of them with the help of floats on her arms. And every few minutes, this dad's cell phone rang and his wife asked, "How are the kids? Is Haley doing ok? You're watching her, aren't you? Don't get so involved in a conversation that you turn your back on her for too long. Make sure she's right in front of you the whole time she's in the pool. It takes only a minute for a child to drown, you know…"

My husband and I could *hear* her chatter to him on the phone from where we were sitting.

This patient husband repeatedly answered his wife's questions, assuring her all was well with the girls. And a few minutes later, she would call him again. After a few calls, he finally shook his head, laughed, and didn't pick up the phone the next time it rang.

Later that evening Hugh said, "Did you hear how she patronized him on the phone? Could you sense how he was being suffocated? That poor guy doesn't stand a chance on his own with his girls. His wife gave him the message loud and clear that she doesn't trust him to take care of his daughters as well as she would. That's *insulting*."

I did feel a little sorry for that dad that afternoon. He was, after all, a great dad. And part of the reason was because he wasn't nearly as uptight about the kids' safety. His children clearly enjoyed being around him. In fact, at one point, one of the daughters spoke up across the pool in an exasperated tone, "Is that Mom checking on us *again*?"

Spare Him the Mothering

One of my friends used to have a habit of calling out "Are you here?" to her husband when she arrived home. It was a matter of wanting to know, as soon as she came through the door, if she was alone or not. (It would be unsettling, after all, for her to assume she was the only one home and then be startled as he walked into the room.)

But one afternoon her husband told her he didn't like her calling out to him, asking if he was home, because it sounded to him like she was checking up on him or wanted to know what exactly he was doing.

"He felt like when I was saying, 'Are you here?' I was really asking, 'What are you *doing* here? Shouldn't you be at work?' Her question, unintentionally, put him on the defensive.

So now when she enters the house she calls out, "I'm home." And if he doesn't answer, she has her answer and knows he isn't there.

Hugh has told me I can give him space by not mothering him and making him account for every single dollar he's spent during the week. (Okay, I *hate* when I do that. And I don't make him account for *every* dollar, but there are some times I will question how many times he's put gas in his car that month or how many visits he's made to Starbucks that week. After all, Hugh has asked me to take care of the budget, and at times I need to know how fast we're going through our money.)

But Hugh says when I question him about dollars and cents, it makes him feel like a child who was given a dollar to buy something from the ice-cream man and he got a little bit of change back and he's being held accountable to come up with the change for his mother. Now, it's not my intention at all to make Hugh feel mothered. But at the same time, to persistently ask about every dollar is to not trust him that he can spend his own hard-earned money wisely. He's right—I *shouldn't* mother him like that.

Spare Him the "No Way Out" Dilemma

Sometimes men simply need to not feel "caged" during a discussion or argument.

Bob said, "Sometimes needing space is a matter of admitting, 'Okay, we've been discussing this problem for too long; let's stop now and relax a bit.'" Giving each other space in the course of a difficult discussion is wise so the conversation doesn't get too intense. There will be times when one of you may need to say, "Let's drop this for now until we can think more clearly." It's better that you agree to take a break, while communicating a desire to eventually work through the problem, than for one of you to end up storming out of the room or clamming up completely because of a need for some personal space.

When He Gets *Too* Much Space

As I write all this, I realize there are husbands who spend more time with friends—or more time alone—than is healthy. Maybe your husband is one of them. Or, maybe he is spending too much time with men who are having a negative impact on his life. If that is the case, ask God to give you wisdom and discernment as to why your husband feels the need to hang out so much or be with those who aren't the best influence for him.

I'm not going to suggest there is an easy fix to such situations. But I do want to comfort your heart with the hope that prayer is your absolute best strategy when it comes to your husband's heart and his priorities. Instead of talking to your husband about your concerns, talk to God first. God knows the heart and mind of your husband even better than *your husband* does, and God can give you that "Holy Spirit wisdom" to know how best to respond.

I also encourage you to gather support around you from other praying wives who are in similar situations. There is no greater support, in prayer and out, than to have your sisters in Christ encouraging you; understanding your concerns; and praying for your perseverance, patience, and unconditional love for your husband. And if his leaving the house to spend unwise time with unwise associations has you burdened, I encourage you to not complain or berate your husband about it. Rather, remain a mystery in what you are thinking, and continue to take your concerns to God in prayer. It's possible that your husband may, because of your reaction—or lack of one—back off from doing what hurts you without you having to say a word.

WHEN A *Woman* INSPIRES HER HUSBAND

From His Perspective

"Men need a band of brothers."

Hugh offers wise counsel here to wives when it comes to understanding a man's need for space.

"Something in the heart of a man yearns for the camaraderie that comes from being with other men. There's a male chemistry, a masculine dynamic that connects us together at our roots. Simply put, a man cannot become all that he is designed to be apart from the involvement of other men in his life. The interaction with women will only bring him so far in this quest to be all things male.

"And it's about much more than just 'hanging out with the guys.' Men uniquely know how to push each other's buttons, the good and positive ones, that dare us to be better than who we know we are and to be more than we think we can become. It's during these times that deep and lasting friendships are forged—forged in the fires of winning a pick-up basketball game or completing a challenging project; of risking nearly everything to see that the right thing was done or said; of earning another man's trust and promising your own; of allowing another man to come face-to face with his fears and failures, knowing that when the dust has settled he is still a man and he still has a friend.

"And it's these friendships that he can turn to when life throws its worst at him, when he doesn't know where else to go and when he begins questioning himself. Then, if he's learned anything at all, he can offer all of that refined strength and trust and resolution of purpose to his wife, who needs her man to come through for her and the family.

"Being around other men also allows a man the freedom to raise his voice and wave his arms if he needs to; to even furrow his brow and become crimson-faced without fearing that someone is going to take it personally."

Men also need time to themselves so they can process what's going on in their lives. Hugh continues:

"If a man doesn't intentionally build space into his schedule to get alone, the pressures of life will eventually undo him. It's not that he has to try and solve all his problems on his own or use time alone as an escape from responsibility, because that will also lead to his undoing. Rather, it has much more to do with giving himself room to breathe, to clear his head and order his thoughts, and to reacquaint himself with who he is apart from the demands and expectations placed upon him by others."

"Who am I, really?" is one of a number of deep questions that arises during those times alone that a man can, or should, wrestle with. And in those solitary places he doesn't have to worry about coming up with the complete answer, as if someone is expecting it in a report due on their desk in the morning. He can revisit those questions as often as he needs to as he spends time alone, hopefully in pursuit of God's wisdom, until the answers become more clear.

"Now let's be clear that when a man enjoys his 'veg time' or just needs to go to his favorite fishing spot for the day, it doesn't always turn into a profound time of life evaluation. More often than not, it is simply for the need to relax and to have a change of pace even for a few hours. 'I miss the smell of the earth' was an entry in my journal that I came across dated October 2008. I remember that I hadn't done any hiking for awhile and my body and soul were craving the outdoors. A few days later I planned out and went on a day hike that rebooted my psyche. And that too is re-invigorating and important to a man's mental health and the care of his spirit."

Mike, who works long hours and has a brutal Southern California commute every morning and evening, says one of the things that speaks loudest to him about his wife's love and appreciation for him is when she helps schedule space for him to enjoy life.

"Working to specifically schedule time for my sporting activities really helps me know she wants me to have downtime that is embraced by her, since this requires her to take on all of the kids during that time."

Did you hear that? Not only does your man *need* his breathing room, but he needs to know you *embrace* the idea of him having some space. He needs to know you're behind him, encouraging him, and even helping him carve out space in his life to decompress, recharge, and enjoy some simple pleasures every now and then. That will mean a lot to him. Be his ventilator, in a sense, and help him find ways to breathe again.

Giving Him the Space He Needs

Okay, I did my research, now it's your turn to do *yours*. After your husband is well rested, or perhaps in an e-mail that he can take time to ponder before he answers, ask him the following questions. (You may want to ask just one question a day so he doesn't feel overwhelmed. Asking him too many questions all at once about how you can give him space will defeat the purpose altogether!)

1. How do you enjoy spending your downtime?
2. What is the best way I can encourage you to do more of that?
3. Are there any ways I might be smothering, mothering, or hovering over you without realizing it? If so, let me know so I can spare you of it. (Make sure you say this one with a smile.)
4. Do you feel you get enough "guy time" in your life? If not, how can I help you make that more of a reality? (And if at this point your husband becomes suspicious and wonders why you are asking, tell him you're reading a book on how to inspire him and encourage him in ways that are best for him. He just might end up giving *you* more uninterrupted reading time!)

A Prayer for You and Your Husband

Help Me Give Him the Space He Needs

God, You are the perfect husband in that You never desire time to Yourself, or time away from me. And yet You made my husband human, and gave him a need to have solitude and time with You alone. Show me, Lord, how to encourage him to take time for himself to do the things he needs to stay healthy and balanced in his life—to spend time with quality men who will help reinforce priorities and values in his life, men with whom he can enjoy healthy, wholesome laughter. On those days that I might tend to resent him for going off somewhere, help me to see that as an opportunity to spend alone with You, my Heavenly Husband, while my earthly husband gets the time he needs to relax, recharge, and re-enter life with me again.

Thank You, God, that You understand my husband's need to be alone, and please draw his heart closer to Yours during his times alone and his times with other men. Help me not to smother, mother, or hover over him, trusting You instead to watch over all he does. In the end, I pray that giving my husband the space he needs will enrich both our marriage relationship and my husband's relationship with You.

> *"The purposes of a person's heart are deep waters, but one who has insight draws them out."*
>
> PROVERBS 20:5

> *"Do what the LORD wants, and he will give you your heart's desire."*
>
> PSALM 37:4 CEV

CHAPTER 6

Encouraging Him to Dream

Do you ever feel threatened by your husband's dreams?

Dave dreamed of retiring and then buying a sports car.

"These weren't *my* dreams," his wife, Kitty, said. "But we looked at cars together and I encouraged him to go ahead and retire, even though I was fearful about how we would survive retirement *plus* have a sports car."

Eventually Dave was able to live his dream. And it turned out to be not as scary as Kitty imagined. He bought a 2002 Miata convertible that they were able to purchase at an exceptionally reasonable price, and a few months later, he retired. "And now," Kitty said, "we enjoy our long drives together under the stars."

"As for retiring," Kitty added, "Dave worked very hard to make sure we would be secure, which we are. Initially I thought it would be hard having him around the house all the time, but we really enjoy our times together. I had to learn to trust my husband's dreams and desires and not stifle him. God has certainly blessed us in this."

Then came the day Dave's friend, Ken, wanted a Miata.

"It's so impractical," his wife, Mary, complained. "And there are other things we need right now. The girls are going off to college soon. I just can't see it."

But Mary *had* promised Ken years ago that if he continued to endure commuter cars while the kids were growing up, he could buy a Miata once he passed down his car to their teenage daughter.

When the time came, though, Mary tried to talk Ken out of it. Kitty and I were there when Mary was stating her case.

"Oh, let him have his Miata," Kitty told Mary. "I didn't think Dave needed one either, but he enjoys it so much and we joined the Miata Club and now riding in that car is something we really enjoy doing together."

Ken ended up getting his Miata, too. And now Mary is glad that he did. "I am happy that driving this car gives him so much pleasure in his daily commute."

I wish I could tell you that my husband, Hugh—also a friend of Dave's and Ken's—was the next to get a Miata. But he wasn't. Hugh, bless his heart, settled for a 2006 Pontiac Grand Prix. We turned in his Ford Explorer because it was on its last legs (or wheels?) and he drove home a two-year-old Grand Prix from the Enterprise Car Rental Sales lot. Although it wasn't brand new, nor was it considered a high-end sports car, it felt that way to Hugh.

Like Kitty and Mary, I had reservations—even about the Grand Prix! I remember telling Hugh, "This car isn't nearly as economical as mine. It doesn't get very good gas mileage. Is a V6 engine really *that* important? And we will probably pay more in insurance just because it *looks* more sporty. And do you need to get the model with power *everything*?" (My little Cavalier has power nothing—crank windows and manual door locks, which forces me to reach across the seats in front and back to manually push down the door locks from inside.)

But just a couple days after driving his "new car," Hugh came through the door and proclaimed, "That is the *newest, nicest* car I have *ever* had. Finally, I can drive a *nice* car."

Hearing Hugh say that—and realizing that as hard as he works and given his income as a pastor, the Grand Prix may be the closest he ever gets to a new car, I was happy for him and regretted my initial reluctance toward his getting the car. As a pastor, Hugh's workload is heavy and filled with stress, and his income allows few luxuries in life. So the low payments we had to make for a two-year-old semi-sports car was a small price to pay for a man who has limited resources for reaching and living out his dreams.

Drawing Out the Dreams

Proverbs 20:5 says, "The purposes of a person's heart are deep waters, but a person of insight draws them out."

I believe a woman of understanding, too, can not only *draw out* the plans and purposes and dreams in the heart of her man, but she can also encourage him to keep dreaming and eventually pursue those dreams as well. On the other hand, I have witnessed many wives, perhaps unknowingly, stifle the dreaming hearts of their husbands.

While sitting outside on a summer evening with "Brandon" and "Denise" (not their real names, of course), Brandon began to dream aloud: "Someday I'd like to own a ranch in Wyoming."

"Really?" Hugh said with a smile and turning toward Brandon. "Tell me about that." But before Brandon could open his mouth and elaborate on a dream deep within him that had dared to sneak to the surface and verbalize itself, his wife shut him down: "Oh, *please*, you've never even ridden a horse! And you want a *ranch*? Where would you *get* a crazy idea like that? And we would never move out of Southern California anyway. We've lived here all our lives." Hugh has since tried to pull the dream out of Brandon, but now, for Brandon, it's a moot point.

eᔭ

"Mark" and "Michelle" were talking with us after church one Sunday. "We're overdue for a vacation," Michelle complained. "Mark's been working hard, but right now is not a good time for him to miss work."

"Actually," Mark said, "I've been thinking a lot about taking some time off and us getting away somewhere," he said, giving her a squeeze. "I love to travel."

"You do *not*," Michelle countered. "We've never gone *anywhere*. How can you love to travel if we've never had a vacation since our honeymoon?"

"Well that's why I'd *love* to travel," Mark said, sounding a little embarrassed and trying to keep the conversation light. "I'm thinking Kauai would be nice, or perhaps a week at Niagara Falls."

"We can't afford that on your income," Michelle responded. "We should just go up north a couple hours and stay with my parents so we don't have to pay for a hotel."

So much for Mark's dream of a romantic getaway with his wife!

⁓

Joy was venting to me about her husband. "Jake has this crazy idea about going wild boar hunting with his brother. It's *ludicrous*," she said.

"It sounds like he's longing for an adventure," I responded. "Men are like that."

"Yeah, but it's dangerous. I'm not gonna let him go off somewhere with his brother for three days where I can't even get a hold of him and then wonder what he's doing and if he's even alive! That would totally stress me out. I told him he needs to think of something more safe and practical."

Don't Be a Dream Destroyer

Yes, a woman certainly has the ability to snuff out her husband's dreams through her fear of what she believes is unsafe, too expensive, or foolish, or through a lack of understanding about the importance of letting a man live out the desires of the male heart. I'm ashamed to admit that, at times, I've been a destroyer of Hugh's dreams, although unintentionally. For me, my reluctance is usually based on concerns for my husband's safety or for our family budget. Maybe you've dampened the dreams of your husband, too, by your response to the verbalization of his dreams, or by not encouraging him to dream in the first place. But it's not too late for you and me to help resurrect those dreams within their hearts and be a helper to our husbands in seeing their dreams through.

"If a husband wants to do something adventurous but doesn't include his wife, it doesn't mean she's any less important to him," Hugh told me. "It just means he wants an adventure."

Whether your husband's dreams sound outrageous, impractical, too expensive, or just too risky, they are nonetheless, his dreams. And a man needs those dreams to help keep his life in focus. We've seen far too many men give up their dreams altogether and settle for what life brings them.

"Too many men are doing something they *have* to do to make money, and not taking the opportunity to do what they really *want* to do when it comes to living from their hearts," my husband told me. As a pastor, he sees many men suffer through burnout or depression because their jobs are draining them of energy and passion. What these men need is something that will reinvigorate them, that allows them to expand their horizons.

"If I'm not careful," one man told me, "I'll spend my entire life working and never doing anything that I've dreamed of. My life will consist of one long resume of work. How tragic. That's why it's important for a man to keep dreaming, and for his wife to come alongside him and give him permission to reach for something *more* in life, even if that something more is as simple and meaningless as a long vacation, a car he's always admired, or a feat he's always wanted to accomplish."

Sometimes those dreams are in the form of adventures that your husband has never experienced and needs to. Deep within his heart is a drive for adventure, a desire to test his limits, a need to engage the deep longings of his masculine soul. Men are all about the adventure—and they sometimes need their wives to affirm those dreams and help make them happen, if possible.

Dreams for a Season

Granted, some of your husband's dreams may last for only a season. We might say it's a phase he is going through. Or maybe some dreams represent challenges that, once accomplished, give your husband a satisfaction that makes him feel ready to move on to something else.

After getting married, Bob dreamed of getting a scuba diving license. His wife, Mary, took a diving class with him. But she ended up hating the activity.

"The equipment was heavy and uncomfortable, and being out in the rough open sea was much different than the quiet environment at the training pool where she took her class," Bob said. "She didn't like going out there. It was unfortunate, and it would've been cool to have a built-in dive partner, but she didn't allow that to discourage me from continuing to dive."

Rather, Mary encouraged Bob to dive with some buddies.

"I think she was happy that she *didn't* have to go," Bob said, laughing about it now. Mary was happy to let her husband live that dream and adventure without her, which he did for a few years. He went on a few more dives, and taught diving classes for awhile. But when he and Mary started having children, he stopped diving and hasn't gone back.

"All through the years that our kids were growing up, I never felt like I missed diving," Bob said. But today, Bob and Mary's adult daughter, Aili, is a world traveler, and she is begging her father to get recertified as a diver so the two of them can dive in Honduras! While Bob's wife wasn't up for sharing the deep sea diving adventure with him, his adult daughter is an adventure girl who is more than ready to accompany dad where he left off in his dream.

Encouraging Him to Dream Big

I once heard a man, in passing, say that a dream is just that—it's something that is out of reach. And therefore there's no possibility of, nor reason for, pursuing it. He called himself a realist. But I call him a cynic. And there's a sense in which I believe the cynicism is indirectly aimed at God, though he might not have intended for that to be the case. I'll tell you why.

God is a big God who makes big dream-like claims in His Word:

- In Genesis 18:14, God said to Abraham, "Is anything too difficult for the LORD?" when his wife, Sarah, laughed at the thought that her dream to have a child would come true when she was 90 years old (NASB).

- In Matthew 7:7-8 Jesus told His followers, "Ask and it will be given to you; seek and you will find; knock and the door will be opened to you. For everyone who asks receives; the one who seeks finds; and to the one who knocks, the door will be opened."

- In Matthew 21:22 Jesus said, "If you believe, you will receive whatever you ask for in prayer." And in John 16:24 He said, "Until now you have not asked for anything in my name. Ask and you will receive, and your joy will be complete."

- In Ephesians 3:20, God is described as the One who is "able to do immeasurably more than all we ask or imagine."

- And in James 4:2, we are told "you do not have because you do not ask God."

Now, God's Word clarifies some of these "ask and it's yours" statements. In James 4:3, we are told, "When you ask, you do not receive, because you ask with wrong motives, that you may spend what you get on your pleasures." (There's the reason God doesn't grant you or your husband's dream to win the lottery!) But when our dreams are similar to God's dreams for us—and do not tear down our bodies, our minds, our hearts, our homes, our marriages, or our relationships— He is pleased to grant them.

Psalm 37:4 instructs, "Delight in the LORD; and he will give you the desires of your heart." The next verse tells us to "commit" our way to the Lord and trust in Him. Those are the conditions He puts around our requests and dreams. In other words, as we put God first, He delights to grant our hearts' desires.

Do you realize that encouraging your husband to dream is not setting him up for failure, but allows him to stretch his faith and enlarge his view of God? And whether he's a believer or not, he needs a big view of God—even if just by seeing your faith that God is the redeemer and restorer and the giver of every perfect gift under heaven.

If you have children, you very much want to give them not only what they need, but what they truly desire, too. How much more does your heavenly Father want to bless *His* children? Matthew 7:11 says, "If you, then, though you are evil, know how to give good gifts to your children, how much more will your Father in heaven give good gifts to those who ask him!"

How can you encourage your husband to dream big? Through this acrostic that spells D-R-E-A-M:

D—*Draw the Dream Out of Him*

When it comes to the dreams on your man's heart, they may be stuffed deep and it may take some creativity and some luring to get them out of him. There may also be some wounds attached to some dreams he's had, especially if they go back to childhood. Maybe he once dreamed of doing something with his father and his father is gone now, so he doesn't talk about it anymore. Or worse yet, maybe he dreamed of something that his dad—or someone else—discouraged him about or made him feel he wasn't up to it. Tread lightly, yet affirmatively. Ask your husband what he'd love to do if time or money were no object. If he's stuck in a practical mode or insists he has no dreams, give it time. And listen for ways that he implies a heart's yearning. It could be something simple like, "I've never been to a pro football game. That would be pretty cool." Encourage him to dream by telling him you'd like to see him achieve his heart's desires so it's about time you start talking about it. And as he shares those thoughts with you, be careful not to be a dream destroyer.

R—*Respond Positively*

Instead of telling him, "Yeah, right, like *that* could ever happen!" be the optimist (and cheerleader) instead: "I think that's a wonderful dream. What could we begin doing now to see that it happens someday?" If his dream seems far-fetched, start praying about it. If it's clearly beyond his reach at this season in your lives, then get creative in ways that can reinforce the dream and keep it alive.

Lisa's husband, Rick, has always dreamed of visiting other countries. So Lisa got creative and started finding a way to honor Rick's dream and to keep him dreaming of what they hope to someday experience together.

"We have monthly date night," Lisa said. "Sometimes I choose a country, go to the library, borrow musical CDs and books to get ideas about that country's clothes, culture, and so on, and then dress for the occasion, decorate accordingly, order take-out, and let him enjoy a 'night in another country'!"

One day Hugh came home from the thrift store with a miniature cottage. I found it on the table. Now, Hugh is not one to collect *things,* so I inquired about it.

"It looks like the cottage I'd like to live in someday," he said. "See all the upstairs windows and the nooks and the little stone walkways around it? I like how it's wooded, too."

I was hearing something from his heart that day—how he dreamed of a warm, roomy, yet quaint place to live in the quiet of the woods. That miniature cottage clearly represents a dream to Hugh. The next day I left Hugh a note saying, "I like your cottage. Let's live in something just like that someday." That little cottage is displayed in our dining room where he can see it—where *we* can see it—and keep his dream alive.

E—*Encourage Him to Take the First Step*

For years Jodi's husband, Troy, has been talking of renting a charter boat and going walleye fishing with his friends. So for his fortieth birthday, Jodi surprised him by booking a six-man charter boat to fish for walleye on Lake Erie.

"I found five of Troy's friends who agreed to go on the trip before I told him about it," Jodi said. Troy, of course, was surprised, but being a very detail-oriented person, he began asking lots of questions. Then he realized that the charter boat was booked, the date was set, and his friends had already agreed to go.

"I think at first Troy didn't like not being in control of making some of the decisions. He asked me how I knew which charter to pick. I had asked several people for their recommendations and then contacted various options before making a decision. Once he was convinced I had done my homework and gotten him a good charter arrangement, he said the trip should be fun.

"The closer the day of the trip came, the more excited Troy got. The lake is about three hours from here, and because the charter boat goes out at six in the morning, they all went to a nearby hotel the night before. Troy liked being able to plan their hotel stay.

"I had encouraged Troy to take some nausea medicine with him. Most everyone I talked to said Lake Erie gets choppy and guys frequently get sick on the boats if they don't take medicine. A bit stubborn, he was the only one who didn't take the medicine—and the only one who was getting sick over the side of the boat!

"Troy said he felt fine after that. The guys caught some fish, but they didn't get the limit, and they didn't catch any big ones. With regard to setting up the trip for Troy I figured that it's the thought that counts, but I also thought the trip hadn't gone as well as they had hoped.

"Recently in the mail, we got a letter from the charter boat captain, who reserved the same Saturday in June for Troy's group this year in case they were interested. I set the letter aside, planning to mention it to Troy but expecting him to decline the opportunity. To my surprise, Troy was kind of excited about going again.

"Sometimes I expect Troy to validate what I do—I want him to act more excited, talk more often, and so on. But his plan to go walleye fishing again makes me feel great. I think he'll enjoy this trip more because he will get to plan it. Which is ironic—in the past he would talk of his desire to go, but he never made arrangements to do so.

"Perhaps he was a bit overwhelmed by the idea of planning such a trip. He's one who plans, analyzes, and fears not making the best decision. Now that he has gone with a charter that he likes, he knows what to expect the next time around and feels confident in selecting that one again. And he said this time, he's definitely taking the nausea medicine!"

While some men might feel a little uneasy about their wives planning their dream *for* them, there are some who might never get out the door if you don't lend a hand—or a push—to help them. Jodi found the balance. She surprised her husband with her gift, which got him started, and has since turned over the helm so he can continue to live out that dream for himself.

A—Acknowledge His Adventure

It is a given that one of your husband's dreams may involve some sort of risk, danger, or adventure. And one of the most discouraging things a man can hear from his wife is "That's too dangerous." Or "Not as long as I'm your wife," or even "You could never handle that." One very important aspect of encouraging your husband to dream is letting him live from his heart. Many times a man will want to do something that doesn't seem safe or practical. And that's when you need to smile, nod, and tell him, "Have a great time, honey."

I remember when Hugh first told me he wanted to climb Mount Rainier. Now, Hugh is an experienced climber who had been to the tops of Mount Shasta, Mount Whitney (twice!), and several Southern California peaks. But I'd also heard the reports of climbing accidents and missing climbers and the deaths that have occurred on Mount Rainier. So naturally I had reservations when Mount Rainier was next on Hugh's list of mountains to scale. He spent a few days, off and on, explaining to me the conditions under which certain kinds of accidents happen and how he was not foolish enough to climb alone, go without proper equipment, or attempt an ascent or descent if the weather wasn't permitting. But finally, when I still didn't relent, he sat me down and said, "I don't need to hear you say, 'Be careful.' That's something my mother would say. I really need you to be excited about this with me and to be confident that your man can accomplish this and to say, 'Hugh, I hope you have a *great* time.'"

Honestly, I thought he was hearing, "I love you and don't want to lose you" in the words "Be careful." Instead, he was hearing, "I don't think you're capable of this, and I'm worried that something will go wrong." I gritted my teeth and tried to sound enthusiastic when I told him, "Have a great time."

And he did. (I won't elaborate on the fact that he was expected back at 5:00 p.m. on a Friday and I didn't hear from him or have any idea of his whereabouts or condition until 2:00 a.m. Saturday, because—in Hugh's words—"The only thing that matters is that I eventually got back in one piece." It turns out that he and his climbing partners couldn't find the path that would lead them down the mountain and had to keep retracing their steps to find it. However, after that incident, he did take out a life insurance policy to protect me financially in case he should ever accidentally die on a mountain!)

Sometimes acknowledging the adventure comes down to the lingo we use. Hugh elaborates: "Men might not freely admit it, but it grates on them when their adventures and activities are described by their wives with words such as 'little' or 'nice.' But that's not the language we speak with other men. We don't say, 'Hey Greg, do you want to grab a little lunch tomorrow?' Or how about 'Yeah, John, Phil and I had a nice little time at the lake.' After all, what guy wants to be *little*? We want to feel big and strong! And the whole 'being nice' thing? Well, we'd much rather be known for being respected, honorable, and a force to be contended with if it ever came down to that. And as we're headed out the door for an adventure with our friends, telling us to be safe, don't get hurt, or be careful sort of kills the moment for us."

Nothing speaks to your husband's male heart more than encouraging him to enjoy his adventure, not tiptoe through it. He doesn't want to be burdened by the thought that you're worrying. And besides, he wants you to be confident he's man enough to handle whatever comes his way. Whatever you do, don't say something motherly like, "If you do something dangerous, I'd be better off not hearing about it," or worse, "If you're not careful, I'll never let you go again!" Instead, say, "Have the time of your life. And I want to hear all about it when you return." What release! What empowerment. And only *you* can empower him that way.

M—Make It Happen, or Make It a Matter of Prayer

Some husbands just aren't planners. They can talk about a dream for years—as Jodi's husband did—but might not have the confidence or knowledge of where to start to make it happen. That's where you might come in, if he's open to letting you help him get there.

Edie's husband, Bill (remember them from chapter 1?), dreamed most of his life of taking a trip to Africa. But to him, it was just that— a dream. When he retired, Edie planned his dream for him. "I wanted to support his dream because I believed that he deserved it after all his hard work." She worked on the details, did the budgeting so they could afford it, and when Bill retired, Edie, Bill, and their two grown sons went to Africa and experienced a real-live safari.

Sometimes your husband's dreams take some organization and planning, and you might be the one who does those kinds of things in your family. I must admit that if I didn't plan our family vacations, we wouldn't have any because Hugh is weighed down with so many details from work that he hardly has time to focus on anything else. So each year I make sure we discuss what he'd like to do during his vacation time—what would help him to relax, and what we need to do financially to make it happen. That makes him feel we are getting closer to the dreams he holds in his heart, some of which are to travel and see and experience different things.

If you do not have the ability or finances to help your husband achieve his dream, then it might be time to lean on God for what only *He* can do. Start praying for open doors that your husband can walk through in terms of his dream. God knows what he needs and what you need too.

Kitty looks back on Dave's dream to retire and buy a Miata and admits that it was God's timing and blessing on their lives that made it happen. They prayed, bringing their requests to God, and watched Him work. Edie, too, cites God as the One who let Bill's dream of seeing Africa fall into place. Now, you might be the only one praying for your husband's dream. If so, keep praying. Remember, you're praying to the God who can do immeasurably more than all we ask or imagine, according to His power that works within us (Ephesians 3:20). In *The Message*, that verse says, "God can do anything, you know. Far more than you could ever imagine or guess or request in your wildest dreams! He does it not by pushing us around but by working within us, his Spirit deeply and gently within us."

Can you be the big dream believer alongside your husband? Can you be the big dream believer *for* your husband? As you encourage him to dream big, he may begin to resurrect some of those deep-seated or lost dreams or begin to believe that he, too, can experience the wonder of a life that is about more than his work.

Don't Assume Your Dream Is Also His

Be careful, my friend, if your husband's dream doesn't appear to be the same as yours. Remember, Kitty didn't share Dave's dream for a Miata, but is now enjoying the fulfillment of that dream with him. The car allowed them to enjoy going out together. Rather than resenting Dave's dream, she worked with him and is now a part of the dream he enjoys. Sometimes it works that way. Other times, you might not share the same dreams or share in their fulfillment. God may have given each of you very *different* dreams, yet you can still enjoy them together by having the attitude that because you love your husband, you support the longings of his heart. If your husband is dying to go somewhere or accomplish something and you truly *don't* want to be a part of that, find a way to let him experience it with your blessing.

Marie saw that her husband's dream looked very different than her own. In fact, his dream looked downright *scary.*

"My husband dreamed of buying a house. When I first saw it, I thought it was the most awful house in the world! It was grungy; it had *squatters* living in it! It was not a nice or livable house. But he was so convinced he could make it our home (not because he loves fixing up homes or even because he wanted a project, but because it was the only house in Los Angeles we could afford!). He had a vision and he really believed that it would be a gorgeous house one day."

Marie let him do it because that's where his heart was—in providing them a home he could afford. She was all smiles when she said, admiringly, "He was *right*. He made this little house into a castle on the hill!"

Hugh and I long dreamed of visiting Israel together, and one spring season, this dream was particularly compelling to him as he was experiencing intense burnout in ministry. But my speaking schedule wouldn't allow us to go during the tour dates that were available. He passed up one tour. Then, regrettably, he started to pass on another tour because I, again, couldn't commit to the dates.

Then I realized, through the suggestion of a friend, that it was more important for *him* to go than it was for us to wait until *we both* could go together. Hugh ended up going on that life-changing trip and returned refreshed and ready to go back to ministry (and back to Israel again with me when the time was right). He considers it one of the most precious gifts I've given him—a time of exploration, meditation, and rejuvenation alone in the lands of Israel, Turkey, and Jordan. He realized the sacrifice I made so he could go. And I saw the trip as something he needed even more than I did at the time.

✑ From His Perspective ✎

"It's all about experience—and leaving a legacy."

Mike is a 42-year-old professional who works long hours, has been married 11 years, and has three young sons. His perspective on dreams amounts to not just wanting to accomplish certain things before he dies, but wanting to leave a legacy for his children as well.

"When I turned forty a couple years ago, I started thinking about how my body's starting to go, and it occurred to me that I might not always be able to do certain recreational things I can do now. Instead of hoping for the red sports car, I started thinking of all the things I wanted to do and hadn't yet done. I also started thinking in terms of a legacy—what do I want my kids to remember about their growing-up years with Dad?

"Men have two choices: You can work full time, or you can work full time. That's really how it is. It's not like it is with our wives, who might have the choice of working full time for a couple years, then having children, then maybe returning to a part-time job as the children grow up. As a man you're always thinking about putting food on the table, and your life becomes so much about work out of necessity that it's important to hold onto some dreams so you enjoy life and remember what matters most. I feel better and healthier when I'm exercising, playing tennis, and getting outdoors recreationally. I'm always trying to think of what I can do with my kids, too."

Mike used to go duck hunting as a child, and now lives in Southern California, where he has very little opportunity to hunt *anything*. He says he still dreams of going wild-game hunting. "I got my scuba diving license recently," he said. "I want to swim with wild dolphins off the coast of Portugal at the Azores Islands in a scuba diving adventure. I'd also like to take my kids scuba diving and snorkeling so we can do those things together."

But his dreams don't end there. "I would also like to swim with some sharks, but likely would use a cage depending on the type of sharks there are. Spear-fishing is also something I'd like to try."

Mike's wife, upon hearing of his dreams to spear fish and go wild-game hunting, laughed affectionately (while cringing at the thought of danger, of course), yet she realizes there is a wild heart within her husband that longs for adventure. She also admires his desire to share some of these adventures with their children.

Therein lies the ability to encourage your husband to dream. Allow him to live from his heart, encourage him to dream big, and keep telling him, "Let's find a way for you to actually be able to *do* that."

❧ Helping Him Pursue the Dream ❧

Is there something your husband dreams of doing that seems a bit risky, expensive, or outlandish? Find out now by following these steps:

1. Start praying through the acrostic D-R-E-A-M on pages 100–106. Ask God to help you draw your husband's dreams out of him, respond positively, and encourage him to take the next step, affirming his adventure and being willing to help make it happen for him.

2. Suggest to your husband that the two of you write out personal goals for the coming year and then discuss them. (You might want to do this each year on your anniversary or on New Year's Day, or even on his birthday. The important thing is to make time to set these goals. Then, a year later, set aside some time and evaluate those goals. That will help you to see whether you're making progress over time, even if minimally so.) Personal goals may include…

   • Places the two of you would like to go to before you die (here's the general dream question).

   • Things the two of you have dreamed of doing that you haven't yet accomplished (that you'd like to try for in the next year).

   • Restaurants, amusement parks, museums, and so on that you'd like to visit in the months ahead.

   • Physical goals such as weight loss, personal accomplishments, and so on.

By doing this exercise with your husband, you are affirming your support for what is important to him and letting him know that you value what he desires in life.

❧ A Prayer for You and Your Husband ❧

Show Me Your Heart for His Dreams

God, thank You for the dreams You have placed within my husband's heart. Give me discernment that helps me to know which dreams are truly from You, and which ones are clearly not in his best interest. Give me a desire to help him experience all You want him to experience, and give me the ears to hear the dreams that work themselves up from his heart and out of his mouth. Help me to be affirming and encouraging in the presence of those dreams.

Lord, the word *encouragement* literally means "to put courage into," and that's what I want to do for my man when it comes to him pursuing and realizing the dreams You have placed in his heart. Help me to be his helper in the true sense of the word when it comes to drawing his dreams out of him, responding to him positively, encouraging him to take the next step, affirming his adventure, and making it happen for him—or trusting *You* to make it happen for him. When it comes to my husband's dreams, may I be the biggest cheerleader he has. And help me to realize that when he begins verbalizing what he longs for, what he's dreamed of, what he truly wishes or regrets, that I am on sacred ground and I must walk carefully to not damage or destroy anything You've put in Your precious son's heart.

Lord, give me the kind of heart for his dreams that *You* have for them.

*"Let my beloved
come into his garden and
taste its choice fruits."*

SONG OF SONGS 4:16

CHAPTER 7

Enticing Him to Pursue

As women, we long to be pursued. We were made that way. It's natural for us, then, as wives, to want our husbands to continue to pursue us—long after our honeymoon.

So why *doesn't* he come after you the way he used to?

I used to think the reason my husband wasn't actively pursuing me was just a matter of the age-old quip "Familiarity breeds contempt." He knows I'm here, he knows I'm available to him, so after a while, it's just no big deal. Then one day I decided I must be doing—or not doing—something that was making him lose interest in me.

Hugh denied that there was a problem. No, he hadn't lost interest in me. No, it wasn't the extra weight I'd gained since my "too-skinny-anyway" days when I'd met him (my rationalization for midlife weight gain). No, it wasn't that his eyes or heart had been lured away by another "mistress" (such as work, or sleep, or a new hobby). For the most part, he said he was often just too drained of emotional and physical energy when he came home from his stressful job to think about anything other than sleep.

But I wasn't satisfied with that. So I started praying about it.

Praying?

That's right.

Isn't it awkward to ask God why your husband is not pursuing you the way he used to? And to show you what you can do to make him pursue you once again?

Not at all. God desires that there be close and fulfilling physical and emotional intimacy between you and your husband. In fact, He wants your husband to be so enamored with you that he sees you as his life's reward. In Ecclesiastes 9:9, King Solomon, with wisdom from God, said this to men: "Enjoy life with the woman whom you love all the days of your fleeting life which He has given to you under the sun; for *this is your reward in life*, and in your toil in which you have labored under the sun."[17]

And in the Bible's book of Song of Songs we read detailed accounts of a husband and wife's physical intimacy and adoration of each other's bodies as God pulls back the curtain for us, with beautiful poetic imagery, on what intimate married life should look like:[18]

> How delightful is your love, my sister, my bride!
> How much more pleasing is your love than wine,
> And the fragrance of your perfume more than any spice!
> Your lips drop sweetness as the honeycomb, my bride;
> Milk and honey are under your tongue.
> The fragrance of your garments is like the fragrance
> of Lebanon.
> You are a garden locked up, my sister, my bride;
> You are a spring enclosed, a sealed fountain.
> You are a garden fountain,
> A well of flowing water
> streaming down from Lebanon (verses 10-12,15).

God delights in the intimacy between a husband and wife, and has designed your husband to long for you physically. So when your man comes after you, he's just being the way God designed him to be—a husband longing for physical connection with his wife. And if he isn't coming after you, there could be a myriad of reasons. I'd like to help you do all you can to make him *want* to pursue you more often.

Now, I take great risk in writing this chapter, out of fear that I may give some of you dear readers the impression that I am implying that you are the reason your husband no longer pursues you. But that is *not* what I am about to tell you. Rather, I am about to point out some reasons your man might not be as sexually interested as he used to (if that happens to be your case).

I also realize there may be some of you reading this who are thinking, *I wish that was my situation. I can't seem to get my husband to STOP thinking about sex. And we've been married for YEARS!* If that's the case for you, keep reading. I'll get to you. But for now, I want to speak to those of you who feel your husband's interests in you might be waning.

When He Doesn't Seem to Notice

Through the years I've had women approach me after a speaking event and ask when I'm going to write a book on what to do about a man's lack of sexual interest in his wife. Some wives are timid and ask this very quietly, believing they are the only woman in the world who suffers from what they perceive as humiliation. Others are more bold, like one woman who said, probably a little too loudly, "I'm sure everyone else in this room has a sex-hound for a husband, but I don't. And he's not old or disabled or anything! How am I supposed to deal with that? How do I let him know I still want that to be a fulfilling part of my life?"

One of the ways we can hurt our marriage—and our husband—is to generalize a situation we're going through and compare it to everyone else's situation. I know that I've done that before. For example, I've read in *Redbook* magazine that the average married couple has sex once or twice a week, and that would make me wonder what's wrong with me or my husband, or *us,* on weeks when we aren't meeting that "quota" and thus being representative of the national average. Or, I'll read to my husband a quote out of a book that speaks of the "intensity of a man's sexual drive" or his "inability to think about anything else when he sees a woman unclothed" and he'll look at me as if he were saying, *Are you asking something? Are you waiting for something? I don't get it.*

So, my friend, please do one thing for me. Right now. Stop comparing your husband to anyone else, and start looking at who *he* is and all that makes up his life—the number of hours he works, his health habits, what he eats, the amount of sleep he gets, whether or not he exercises, the pressures he faces, the projects he's working on, and add to those factors his age, his medical history, any medications he is taking, and his physiological makeup, and you have one man with about a *billion* reasons for why he might not be meeting the so-called "national average" when it comes to how much he is—or is not—pursuing you sexually. In other words, don't take it personally.

Now that I've said that, because you have picked up a book on how to inspire your man and you've read this far, I'm assuming you want to know more about how you can get your husband to pursue you. So we're not going to talk about what *he* can do differently (or tell him that if he exercised more or ate better, he would have more energy for sex!). Instead, we're going to talk about *you* and your approach to his desire—or his seeming lack of desire—for you.

Maybe He's Been Burned

Sometimes your husband's lack of motivation to pursue you might come down to his fear of rejection. Perhaps he's been burned. If you've ever brushed off his advances (and who of us hasn't when we have children in the room, work to finish, deadlines to complete, dinner to cook, laundry to fold, or just a million other things on our mind?), then he has already experienced the risk and resulting humiliation of you telling him no. And that may be why he refuses to take that risk again. He may figure, "I've initiated so many times, I'm not going to anymore. If she's interested, she'll come after *me* for a change."

As much as a woman can feel hurt when she experiences rejection by her husband, a man can feel that wound even more intensely.

Author and marriage expert Dennis Rainey says, "Most men find initiating the sex act one of the riskiest ventures he could ever make.

Why? Each time he initiates sex, he risks rejection." Rainey goes on to say, "When a man is rejected often enough, he typically internalizes his anger, his hurt, and his disappointment until such time when the rejection drives him to one of several reactions—none of them are good. Either he will give up on the relationship, he will seek alternative sexual outlets such as pornography, or he might compromise his wedding vows by pursuing female affirmation elsewhere."[19]

Can you see how very important you are when it comes to your husband's need to feel affirmed as a man sexually? It isn't a desire or need based on selfishness. It is a *normal* desire and need. He was created that way. Rainey continues, "Your husband's sexuality is so much a part of who he is that it affects virtually every part of his life. The wise woman understands that her man longs to be needed sexually by her. If you really want to get to the bottom line for men, and you really want to express love to your husband in a powerful way, just express to your husband that you need him sexually."

I think Rainey's words convict the heart of *every* wife who has ever shunned her husband's advances or rolled her eyes, thinking, *Not that again!* To love our husbands is to want to affirm them not just with our words, but with our actions and our attitudes toward them as well, including in the realm of sex.

If the scenario described above sounds like your situation at home, then it may be time for you to go overboard—or maybe start in small ways—to let your husband know you desire him physically as well as emotionally. And if you feel you have worn out the discussions on why he isn't interested in sex—or *you*—then it might be time for a different approach.

Maybe He Needs a "Boost"

With age comes inevitable loss. Loss of (or decreasing) memory, loss of energy, loss of hair (except in some cases for women, who get *more* hair in places where we *don't* want it!), decreasing metabolism, and—for men, especially—decreasing testosterone levels. It's just a fact. A man's sexual drive decreases as he ages. So in many ways, the roles reverse as we get older. He initiated back when you first got married, back when you needed a long time to warm up and get in the mood. Now that his testosterone level has decreased, he may be the one who needs help with the "warm up." That's where you come in.

Remember the days you thought long and hard about what to wear, how to do your hair, even what to say when you were around him? You wanted to make the best impression on him so he would ask you out again. Deep inside, you wanted him to love you for who you *are*. But first he needed to fall in love with what he saw.

That's the way we are as women. We very much want to attract the man whom we will eventually marry. So why, then, do we get *offended* at times when our husbands still want us, today, to look like we did back then? So it was okay to attract your husband before marriage, but once the deal was consummated, he shouldn't care about your looks anymore?

As one marriage and family therapist says, "When we're dating, we're flirty. We do our hair all cute and wear cute clothes. We are appealing to their sexual desire. But when we get married, we resent their sexual desire. We expect them to just love us for who we are inside."

Well, of course our husbands should love us for whom we are inside. But they are still very visually oriented when it comes to their sexual drive. Males are naturally attracted to the beauty, softness, and sex appeal of females. So be the woman he loves to look at just as much as you once were.

Debbie said of her and Marvin's marriage, "Our relationship is so close that having eyes only for each other is relatively easy. However, he 'practices' having eyes only for me—which is something he regularly commits to in prayer." In addition to relying on Marvin's integrity as a man of God, Debbie wears her hair long for him, tries to dress to please him, and gives him lots of attention and touches him frequently. And, she adds, "I never turn him down, regardless of how I feel."

As I mentioned in the first chapter, your husband wants to enjoy sexual activity and pleasure with *you*. And you are the only one he can enjoy that with and know that he is right and pure before his God.

When wives withhold themselves sexually from their husbands, they are quite possibly allowing their husbands to be tempted sexually and more susceptible to opening a door that is prohibited to them. Believe me, your husband does not want to stray from you emotionally or physically. Yet sexual temptation can be a huge problem in men's lives simply because of how they are visually and physically wired. Inasmuch as it depends on you, don't even let a door crack open to make him think about how he might satisfy that built-in craving with anyone other than you or in any other way.

All of that to say, sometimes your husband needs a boost—a boost to his ego so he will believe you want him physically as well as emotionally. And a boost to get him in the mood to connect with you physically. Sometimes he needs some extra effort on your part to be enticed and drawn toward you. Just as there are a myriad of reasons he might seem to have lost interest in you, there are also a myriad of ways (or at least 26—one for every letter of the alphabet) to recapture his interest and make him want to pursue you again. Here is the start of what I call the ABCs of making you irresistible in his heart and eyes.

A—*Affirm Him*

As I mentioned in chapter 2, one of the things your husband finds most attractive about you is that you were at one time (and hopefully still are) attracted to *him*. A man wants to be around a woman who makes him feel like he's winning.

My friend Marie said, "I make sure to take time to tell my husband how proud I am of him. I tell him how much his hard work pays off and helps our family. I remind him that there is no one like him out there. I remind him that he makes me feel safe and loved." All of those things, she said, personally affirm a man. They tell him he is cutting it as not only a man, but also as a husband. Let him know he's still hot, he can still get your heart racing, he still looks good, he's a great provider, he is great at what he does—whatever it is that you can compliment him on. And mean it. A woman who sings his praises is a woman he'll come after...so he can hear more!

B—*Be a Mystery*

Men love a challenge—just don't make it *too* complicated. Does your husband know everything there is to know about you? If so, develop a new skill or idea or come up with a secret he's dying to discover. When you become a mystery to your husband there will be things about you that he wants to know, things he would like for you to divulge, secrets in your soul that he'll be challenged to draw out. You don't give him a chance if you tell him *everything*. Surprise him with little "secret admirer" notes at times he doesn't expect them. Offer to meet him somewhere and show up in a new dress and hairstyle. Be mysterious and surprise him in ways you know he will enjoy. Be to him a treasure chest full of secrets he's dying to unlock!

C—*Cultivate Your Relationship with Christ*

What makes you truly attractive and one worth pursuing? The beauty of Christ in you. When you have an intimate devotional life with Christ and are controlled by His Spirit, your life will produce the fruit of His Spirit—love, joy, peace, patience, kindness, goodness, faithfulness, gentleness, and self-control (Galatians 5:22-23). What man *doesn't* want to chase after a woman who is truly joyful, peaceful, patient, kind, good, faithful, gentle, and—they love this one the best—self-controlled!

D—*Dress for Him*

Some women don't think much about what they wear, and give the excuse that they're just not into the latest fashions. Or, they will dress nice when they go to church, or out with girlfriends, but not put much effort into how they look for "just my husband." But men *can* recognize "frumpy" even if we can't. Rhonda said, "I feel like it's a betrayal to my husband to work hard to look my best when I am going out but not make the same effort for him when we are just going to stay at home together." And dress for him at night too. Your husband might be majorly turned off by a "grandma" nightgown that resembles something his mother used to wear. So it may be time for you to invest in new lingerie or something "form flattering" or feminine. Rhonda said, "I am a firm believer in purchasing new lingerie from time to time. It doesn't have to be expensive; just something fresh and exciting."

E — Exude Confidence

He once found it attractive in you. He still does. So regardless of how you might feel about your weight, body shape, "big knees," "small chest," cellulite, veins, or *whatever,* get over it. He has. Honestly, he doesn't see all the body flaws you think are so very obvious. He doesn't analyze or critique your body *nearly* as much as you do. In fact, male eyes are pretty forgiving and "blind" when it comes to our overexaggerated flaws, especially when you agree to turn the lights on during intimate moments (try keeping the light low—it gives your skin a nice glow and your body a "soft focus"). And when you are confident in your speech, your walk, your relationship with him, and your role as his wife, that too is attractive. Be confident in who you are as a woman, and that will also make you a mystery.

F — Flirt with Him

If he loved it back then, your husband will still love it today— maybe even more. Flirting is a hidden art among married women today. We usually have too many other things on our mind to even think about saying something to get his attention and let him know we're thinking of him. My friend Kathi Lipp, author of several books, including *The Husband Project* and *The Marriage Project,* said, "Flirting is so not talking to him about all the things we have to get done around the house. It's more like reminding him of something I admire in him or telling him he is great at something. It's a lot like being the cheerleader again and seeing him as the football star."

Remember our discussion in chapter 2 about how a man— in midlife—needs his wife to be his cheerleader, not his mother? A mother coddles him, scolds him when necessary, and tells him what time he'd better be home for dinner. A cheerleader smiles and winks at him, laughs at his jokes, and cheers him on regardless of how the game is going (while wearing a short skirt, of course!). Now which, do you think, is more appealing to a man?

Michelle flirts by texting her husband love messages while he is at work. "Texting is a much safer means, I found out one morning," Michelle told me. "One day I telephoned my husband at work to call him sexy and let him know how much I enjoy him. He laughed and then quickly picked up the phone. Unknown to me, he had a coworker sitting there listening to my sweet-nothings message on speakerphone!" Granted, Michelle was more embarrassed than her husband. I'm sure around his office he was *the man* that day with quite a wife—and a *wild* one at that!

G—Give Him the Best of You

We tend to give the best of ourselves to our jobs, our children, our homes, and sometimes even our pets. And our husbands tend to get the leftovers—of our time, energy, and even our looks.

I know many women who enjoy remodeling their homes. Remodeling the bedroom. Remodeling the bathroom. Changing the colors, giving it a lift with some new paint. Moving the furniture. Switching it up. Out with the old, in with the new. They enjoy putting a fresh face on something—to give it a lift or a new look.

But what about remodeling ourselves now and then?

The Bible says our bodies are the temple of God. So how long has it been since the temple's been remodeled?

Now I'm not talking about plastic surgery, body enhancements, or botox! (And living in Southern California, which is the plastic surgery capital of the world, I *do* see a lot of it.) I am talking about doing what we can to keep our bodies in shape, healthy, and holy for our Lord and for our husbands.

First Peter 3:3-4 tells me that I need to not *only* be concerned about external beauty, but with the "inner self, the unfading beauty of a gentle and quiet spirit, which is of great worth in God's sight." We are called to have an attractive spirit, an inner beauty. And yet we shouldn't use that as an excuse to say, "It's only what is inside that counts." It isn't *all* that counts. Your husband still needs to find you attractive. Just as we don't want to ignore our inner beauty by concentrating too much on our outward beauty, so we don't want to ignore our *outer* appearance while claiming the spiritual is all that matters. Men truly want *both*.

The Bible tells us that we are not only the temple of God, but we belong to our husbands. So we need take care of ourselves for *them* too.

H—Have a Positive Attitude

Dan said what he finds most attractive about his wife, Debbie, is that "her mood and demeanor are almost always pleasant and positive. I can always count on a smile or kind word. I never ever worry about what kind of mood she is in." Can your husband always count on a smile or a kind word? Or does he enter the house walking on eggshells, unsure of what kind of mood you'll be in? Positive people are enjoyable to be around. If you're pleasant, your husband will enjoy being in your company.

I—Initiate

I can't say enough here. Initiate a hug. Initiate a kind word or compliment. Initiate lovemaking. Chances are your husband dreams of the "wild woman" within you. Let your inner tigress come out now and then and show him he's still the one. You want to be pursued. So does he every now and then. Surprise him. And show him there's a side of you he has yet to discover.

"Sarah" recounted an intimate conversation her husband had with her years ago: "My husband once told me, 'I want *you* to be my fantasy girl. I don't ever want to fantasize about anyone else. So can I be safe coming to you with what I need and long for sexually?'" Fortunately, Sarah was moved by his honesty rather than offended by it. And she responded enthusiastically by telling her husband she'd be more than happy to be his one and only fantasy girl. Good for her! Most husbands would *love* for their wives to initiate lovemaking—so try it, and become the fantasy girl he desires for you to be!

J—Join Him in Something He Enjoys

Michelle—who gave her husband an office thrill when she "complimented" him while he was on his speaker phone—said she became more of a pursuit to her husband when she adopted his interest in working out.

"I was complaining to my husband that I was tired, bored, and didn't have time to exercise. He told me that the kids were always going to take my time, and that I was the only one who could make working out a priority. I started to listen. I made time for my workouts a priority. I made the kids ride their bikes while I started running. Now, years later, I'm not the nagging, tired old wife. I am the *new* wife, with a cute body, and more interesting things to talk about. We talk about workouts, nutrition, and even exercise together. It has really ignited a new passion within our marriage. I can't keep up with my husband, but the fact that I try makes it more interesting."

By taking up an interest that her husband had, Michelle was able to accomplish nearly every one of the ABCs simply by carrying out the letter J. (You can download the complete list of the ABCs—through the letter Z—by clicking on "Resources for Couples" or "Free Resources" on my Web site at *www.StrengthForTheSoul.com*. Now you're gonna *have* to take a look at that list to know what I came up with for Q, X, and Z, aren't you?)

Finally, I must add that because we're talking about our husbands in this chapter, you may want to go back and add the phrase "in the bedroom" to every suggestion listed in A-J above. (Go ahead…try it… pencil the phrase in after each point and you'll see what I mean.) After all, when it comes to some people, money talks. But when it comes to husbands, in general, sex talks—and rocks, from their point of view!

From His Perspective

"I find her differences attractive."

When I asked husbands to tell me what they found most attractive in their wives, physically and emotionally, I was encouraged to see that they weren't all looking for a size 4 woman with curves. In fact, none of them were. They were looking for the woman they fell in love with, and anything that still resembled her today. And they love the way you are different from them. Listen to their responses:

- My wife keeps herself in shape, which tells me she still cares about wanting to look good for me.

- I like that my wife and I enjoy doing similar things. I love that she can be spontaneous when we need to be. She's willing to drop whatever she's doing and go do something else when we need to.

- I love her attitude. It's always pleasant and positive.

- I'm attracted by what she knows, her natural talents, her ability to have a conversation. She's most attractive when she is doing the things she loves to do.

- My wife is dependable and I'm attracted to her steadfastness, the fact that I can count on her.

- I'm attracted to my wife's "whole package." She has not let herself go. She considers her appearance important. She still looks like the woman I dated. I appreciate that.

- My wife is very nice and gracious and loving toward others. She always has a nice answer for people and never talks negatively about anyone. She's soft, and she rarely hurts anyone with her words or actions.

- My wife is committed to me. She hasn't ever considered that we wouldn't solve a problem together. That is very attractive.

One husband, married just over 10 years, summed up what I believe all husbands think, at one time or another, about their wives. He said, "I find her differences attractive." Hear his words and draw confidence from who you are and ways you are helping—and being attractive to your husband—that you might not even realize: "All the things I find attractive about my wife stem from one thing: her ability to do things *I can't* do. I rely on her a lot to help me be a more functional person, and as I get older, I better understand what I am pathetic at and what I need her to help me with. So her ability to do things like shop for people, remember birthdays, cook, dress herself and me well, make the house a home, be nice to people, smooth over social situations where I put my foot in my mouth, meet people at parties, keep in touch with friends—those are functional things she can do and I can't. Her talents also make her attractive to me. Once again, things she can do that I can't—like dance."

Chances are, there are quite a few things you can do that your husband can't. And maybe he hasn't verbalized that to you yet, but nonetheless, it's a part of you that is attractive to him because it's a part of you that he *needs*.

Another husband alluded to the male-female differences when he told me what he found most attractive in his wife: "One of the most profound things that continues to attract me is that my wife is an unsolvable intrigue—I can't predict how she will feel or react in certain situations because it depends on what she is experiencing in many areas of her life and relationships. This challenges me to search how I can be the type of husband to help meet a portion of her emotional needs. This unpredictability, while burdensome at times, actually challenges me at the deepest level of the relationship to pursue her as a love interest."

So you wish your husband completely understood you? Relax. Maybe your husband is like the one above, who finds the feminine mystique in you alluring.

Shine, my friend, and exude the confidence that comes from being a woman as unique and as different as you are. It is one of the things that make you truly attractive—and enticing—to your man.

∾ Let the Pursuit Begin ∾

Ask your husband what three qualities about you attracted him the most when you first met or got married, and list them here. (Encourage your husband to answer honestly and not be afraid of how you might react. And please don't imply anything negative from his answers if they sound like qualities that date from long ago.)

1.

2.

3.

How can you cultivate those three qualities in your life on a more regular—or even daily—basis so that you are putting into action the things that first attracted your husband to you?

Take time to finish the rest of the ABCs that I started for you in this chapter. Can you think of additional ways to draw your husband's attention to you? Come on, get creative. Chances are you'll come up with better ones than I have listed. And please email them to me at *cindi@strengthforthesoul.com* so I can include your great suggestions as another free resource for wives on my Web site.

✐ A Prayer for You and Your Husband ✐

Lord, Light that Fire in Me

Heavenly Father, in Song of Songs 4:16 the bride said to her lover, "Let my beloved come into his garden and taste its choice fruits." Lord, would You cultivate within me the same perspective so that I will continue to attract my husband to myself and entice him to pursue me? You gave me to him as a gift, and I want to continue to be his greatest gift today. Help me to see that my role as his partner also includes being his lover and the woman he can safely and righteously live out his male sexuality with. Help me to see our intimate moments as another way I can minister to him. Help me to eagerly pursue him as a way of showing him I love him and need him. Lord, light that fire in me so I can re-ignite that fire in him.

"A wife should put her husband first, as she does the Lord. A husband is the head of his wife, as Christ is the head and the Savior of the church, which is his own body. Wives should always put their husbands first, as the church puts Christ first."

EPHESIANS 5:22-24 CEV

CHAPTER 8

Letting Him Lead

I can't tell you how many times I've heard a woman criticize her husband's ability to lead. Whether he's failing, in her eyes, to be the spiritual head of the household or just not appearing to want to take the lead in parenting, budgeting, or planning the family vacations, many wives believe their husbands are passive.

I've learned now to ask the obvious—but sometimes uncomfortable—question: Have you ever *let* him lead?

"Basically, men lead best in their homes when their wives *let* them," said Bob, who has been married 35 years and teaches a married couples' Bible class. "Wives need to know how to step back and acknowledge that their husband has an opinion that is as valid as theirs."

Bob—and my husband, who has 20 years' experience as a pastor—have seen husbands shut down many times because their wife has jumped in and taken the lead, whether it be in a class when they are called upon for input, or in the home, where there isn't any room for them to be the head of the family.

Then there are some men who don't shut down. Instead, they will go head-to-head with their wives. But they don't want to go through that power struggle. They want to lead as a way of ministering to their wives, and so their wives will not feel the burden of having to do the leading themselves.

In his book *Sacred Influence,* author Gary Thomas says, "The typical man remains unmoved by power plays or criticism or by a wife who disrespects him. He's moved by a wife who lets him lead and then helps him get where he wants to go.

"This isn't merely cultural. Neuroscience has shown this is how men's brains are wired. Men, for the most part, are physiologically inclined toward certain attitudes at work and home. If you really want to move your man, you must treat him the way God designed him to be treated."[20]

This is particularly challenging if you are as much of—or more of—a leader than your husband.

Mike, who has been married 11 years to a very capable wife, said, "My wife is a take-charge woman, and quite frankly, that is the only type of woman that attracts and interests me. The drawback is that she can be overcontrolling at times, which can lead to frustration for me and the kids.

"We both want to develop the same character qualities in our children, but our methods and communication styles are quite different. I think she can find that God would use her husband in more special ways to alleviate her burden of controlling the household by *giving* me more space to lead the home."

That we as women can slip into the mode of leading in our homes is understandable. We love our husbands and children and we want the best for them. But we can easily forget God's design for the husband and wife in the home, which we'll talk about in this chapter. And we can forget that our "dark side" is showing when we, in the depths of our hearts, believe we can lead better than our husbands can.

The desire to take over in our homes is built into every wife as a result of the curse placed in Eve after she sinned in the Garden of Eden. Now please stay with me here: This is meant to *enlighten* you, not chastise you, so that you understand where your frustration comes from when you feel your husband *isn't* leading in the way that you'd prefer.

Blame It on Eve

In Genesis 3, we read that Eve succumbed to the serpent's temptation to disobey God and eat of the forbidden fruit. Then she took it upon herself to suggest that her husband, Adam, do the same. When he in turn followed, God punished all three of them. The serpent had to eat dust and crawl on his belly all the days of his life. Adam and all men after him would have to work the land, which was cursed with thorns, in order to make a living. And Eve would not only have her pain multiplied in childbirth, but her "desire" would be for her husband and he would rule over her.

Now, that "desire" was not referring to Eve's emotional or sexual desire for her husband. Rather, she would long for his position of authority.

We know that because when God said to Eve, "Your desire will be for your husband, and he will rule over you" (Genesis 3:16), He used the same Hebrew word for "desire" that is used in Genesis 4:7. There, God confronted Eve's son, Cain, after the murder of his brother, and said, "Sin is crouching at the door; and its *desire* is for you, but you must master it."[21] That Hebrew word for "desire"—in both verses—refers to an unhealthy desire that could bring about destructive results.

Thus, as a result of the fall into sin, you and I are cursed with a *destructive desire* to take the lead from our husbands.

Maybe you're thinking at this point, *But somebody has to lead in my home.* Well, that somebody is your husband. Many times he just needs to be allowed—or encouraged—to lead. There will be times he makes mistakes. He won't always get it right. But that doesn't mean he has been disqualified from leading. After all, do *we* get it right every time?

I realize it may be difficult, at times, for you to let your husband lead—especially if you are a get-it-done woman who tends to accomplish things at a different pace than your husband. And the better you are at getting certain things done, the more difficult it may be for you to stand back and let your husband lead—at work, at home, in your ministry, in your marriage, in his parenting, and so on.

But here is what I've found by interviewing numerous husbands:

They want a *partnership* with you. They want to work *with* you on the decisions that affect their job, their marriage, their family. They value your opinion; they just don't want you lording things over them. They *want* your advice; but they also want you to ask for *theirs* too. They sometimes don't know how to best handle a situation, but they also feel a tension within because they still feel responsible to lead. So they want your input—and your trust—when it comes down to the two of you going with a decision he has made.

What Leading Looks Like to Him

Your husband needs your respect. And one of the best ways to show your respect for him is to value his ability to lead.

"My husband and I had a difficult relationship issue with our extended family," Alice told me. "He felt he needed to take a certain action to be a person of integrity. I said 'Okay, I'll be on board with you.' The fact that I supported my husband, even though I disagreed with how he felt the situation should be handled, really meant a lot to him. But bottom line is this: If he feels strongly about it, I'm on board."

(Is it any wonder Alice is the cheerleader I mentioned in chapter 2?)

For you, the idea of letting your husband lead might be equivalent to holding up a white flag of surrender and letting everything descend into chaos around you. But as I said earlier, your husband doesn't want you to go dormant and leave him out there on his own. He wants a partnership with you. He wants to work *with* you. He wants you to be *on his team*, not at his beck and call.

Consider the viewpoint of husbands and what it looks like in their homes when their wives let them lead:

- "Ask me for opinions and input on decisions."

- "Don't assume I am always going to agree with your ideas or suggestions. Be willing to adjust or re-arrange your ideas so they are more in line with mine."

- "Ask, 'What do *you* think?' 'What would *you* like to do?' 'Do what you think is best—I trust you,' and really mean it."

- "If I make a decision and it flops, don't chastise me or berate me for it—we all make mistakes. Talk about how the situation can be turned around or recovered. Think in terms of solutions, because that is how my work world operates."

- "You can let me lead by valuing my opinion, telling me you trust me, telling me your needs, bringing your concerns to me in a constructive way, making suggestions rather than demands, and respecting my point of view in front of others, especially the kids."

Bob, a Bible class teacher who has been married 35 years, offers this insight on what it looks like for him to lead in his marriage and in his home: "I enjoy being able to talk over problems with my wife. A man leads best in the home when he can stand with his helpmate and discuss things. We husbands don't always have the answers. Half the time I don't. But when we put our heads together, we can arrive at the best possible solution."

That is partnership—you coming alongside your husband to solve problems or make decisions. Not dumping something in his lap and saying, "You figure this out!" and not running ahead and being the CEO without his consultation. And the beauty of partnership in a marriage is that you and your husband can bring your different perspectives, ideas, and ways of thinking together to examine something and come up with the best possible solution or decision.

"Women have a tendency to function with their whole brain, rather than just the left or right side," Bob said. "That's why 'together' is the ideal mode for discussing and deciding on things. We husbands and wives have a tendency to take sides, thinking our own particular way is the best solution.

"Wives tend to ask their husbands to go ahead and lead because they know they should do that, but at the same time, deep down inside, they think they already know the answer. But it's important to consider the answer your spouse has, for it might help bring you both toward an even better solution."

Why should a woman be willing to come alongside her husband as a helper when it comes to decisions?

"We don't always make the best decisions at times," Bob said. "We can benefit from input. But we don't need our wife to dominate and take over."

Steve said, "I love my wife's ability to think differently; it makes me feel like we make better decisions because we come at our problems from two completely different angles. Of course that can be problematic at times, but in the long run it's better. It means we've covered every angle. And that makes me feel better."

When your opinion differs from your husband's, it doesn't have to result in an argument. Offer your thoughts as an opportunity to put something else on the table. Then see what your husband or God might do with those thoughts. If your husband doesn't go along with it, then your reaction is key to what happens next.

Knowing When to Back Off

There may be times when your man is just as capable as you when it comes to dealing with a situation, but he isn't able to verbally express himself as well. Or perhaps his thinking process is different than yours because of his personality, upbringing, or the way he generally works his way through matters. That's when you need to know when to lighten up or back off altogether.

"My wife is much more confident in her decision-making process than I am," Bob said. "So when we discuss certain problems, generally speaking, I'm coming from a less secure position than she is. When we discuss situations in the home, she knows when I'm feeling less secure, so she will step back and let me say as much as she has said, and she does that to give me the opportunity to lead."

The admonition to let our husbands lead is clearly stated in Ephesians 5:21-24:

> Submit to one another out of reverence for Christ. Wives,
> submit yourselves to your own husbands as you do to the

Lord. For the husband is the head of the wife as Christ is the head of the church, his body, of which he is the Savior. Now as the church submits to Christ, so also wives should submit to their husbands in everything.

I love how biblical counselor Elyse Fitzpatrick says it: "Submission to your husband flows out of your sincere, faith-filled submission to the Lord."[22]

Rather than get into the "but I'm not just a doormat" argument, I want to put the emphasis on selflessness—on the way Christ asks us to follow Him.

The exhortation in Ephesians 5:22 to "submit to your husbands *as to the Lord*" makes it clear that following our husband's lead and submitting to him, when it comes down to who has the last say, is a *spiritual* issue. *Your* spiritual issue, not your husband's. In other words, we women are not told, "Submit to your husbands only when they are acting like Christ." Rather, we are told to follow their lead just as we would follow Christ's. Even if your husband is not leading you as Christ would (and I know we can play that card, at times), we are still to yield to our husband's lead in the same way that we surrender our will and follow the lead and authority of Christ.

Just like men, we as women were created in the image of God. That means we too are naturally able (because we are made in God's image) to rule, oversee, manage, and administrate. We need those traits in order to parent our children, right? And in order to coordinate our family's social events and activities, or plan the family reunion, or head up the project at work, or lead that ministry at church. Many wives are more than capable of leading. We just need to know where and when to back off and let our husbands shine.

I realize that as you read this, you might be feeling very frustrated. Maybe even a little bit hurt. You are leading by default. You are leading because your husband won't lead. Or you are leading because you feel your husband doesn't know how to lead.

This is where I want you to open your heart to an idea that God may want to speak into your heart just about now. Would you start to pray as you read these next few paragraphs?

Give Your Man a Break

Your husband may be fearful of leading, of making the wrong decision, of not cutting it when it comes to your—or his family's—expectations. If that is the case, that is where he needs your partnership, your prayer, and your praise.

I know many women who have become bitter because they are leading their families spiritually by default.

"My husband won't make our kids go to church, so I do," one woman complained to me. "I give them daily devotions, I pray with them at night, I'm the one who brings up spiritual values and discussions in our home. Why can't *he?*"

Let me point out that setting up family devotions every morning is not the ultimate test of whether your husband is leading his home spiritually. Hugh and I know plenty of individuals who grew up with daily family devotions but didn't necessarily see godly leadership in their homes. One doesn't necessarily equate to the other. A man can give spiritual leadership in all kinds of ways just by the interaction he has with his children, whether it be through discipline, guidance, or just conversation. If he is pointing his children to Christ and to Scripture, then he is providing spiritual leadership. That leadership doesn't have to be in the format of a Bible study. So we, as wives, need to put aside our expectations of what spiritual leadership looks like and begin to see our husbands for who they are, individually, and how they may *already* be expressing their faith in ways that we have perhaps missed or didn't deem as being spiritual (more on this in the next chapter).

Now I want you to think about something for a moment: What if God gave *you* the role of spiritual leader? What if He made *you* responsible and accountable for the spiritual condition of your family? Perhaps you feel He has because your husband isn't following Christ or he isn't initiating the spiritual development of your marriage or family. But because of the command in Scripture for the husband to be the head of his wife, and therefore, ultimately, the head of his home, your husband carries that burden more than you do. Can you imagine the weight on his heart that comes from knowing that every morning as he wakes up (and probably has to head out to a job) and every evening as he goes to bed (possibly exhausted from all he's had to do that day) and every moment that he gets a report on how one of his children is doing, he is accountable to God for how he is directing and leading his family?

As mothers (if you're a mother reading this), we already take on much of the burden for how our children are developing spiritually. But wouldn't it be intimidating if our God-given role was to be the spiritual head of the household? (Even if you're thinking, *Well, I already am the spiritual head by default,* you still have the affirmation in your heart that God is pleased with all you are doing because your husband isn't doing those things. But what if that were your obligation? And you felt not quite up to the task?)

I will admit that there are times when I am a lousy role model in my own home—to both my husband and our daughter. There are days when I think about myself first, and I don't realize it until after I've been ugly to one or both of them. And although I serve a gracious and forgiving God, I am still accountable to Him for my actions. I must still confess the times I blow it and agree with God that I was wrong and I so need Him to control my every thought, word, and action. Yet if I had to live with the pressure that God was going to hold me accountable for the bottom-line spiritual health of my entire family, I wonder if I'd buckle at the pressure.

I would probably constantly feel I was blowing it.

Do you wonder if your husband ever feels that way? Men hate to feel that they have let someone down or disappointed someone who was counting on them. If he *is* blowing it (from your perspective), believe me, he probably already knows that and therefore feels even worse about himself. In his eyes, he's disappointed you, his family, *and* God.

Hugh and I heard a national speaker—who was a man, by the way—state his personal opinion that because Adam didn't man up in the Garden of Eden and keep his wife from eating that dang forbidden fruit, every man after him has borne the shame (and ongoing guilt) of not being the spiritual leader that he should be in his marriage. While that is admittedly an opinion, I have often wondered if that's the case—if men still bear the shame of having not been a strong leader in the situation that caused the downfall of the human race. I mean, think about it. Adam blew it in Eden by not keeping his wife from giving into temptation. He *followed* her into sin, rather than protecting and preventing her from falling into sin.

Scripture *doesn't* say that after Eve ate of the fruit, "she also gave some to Adam and convinced him it was okay to eat of it, but he declined, saying, 'Oh dear, what have you *done?*'" No, Scripture says, instead, that Eve "gave some to her husband, *who was with her,* and he ate it" (Genesis 3:6, emphasis added). Adam was standing right there! He failed God *and* his wife by letting her disobey God and then following her in that disobedience. Instead of putting his foot down and dealing with the serpent directly, and saving his wife and himself from carrying out actions that would ultimately lead to the curse of all mankind and the earth, he defied God and fell into sin. And Romans 5:12 makes it very clear that all of us inherited sin from Adam: "Sin entered the world through one man, and death through sin, and in this way death came to all people, because all sinned."

So that national speaker's comment does seem to make sense—that one result of the curse is a man's inner sense of self-condemnation that he is not up to the task of leading his wife and family. Then add to that a wife who believes her husband is constantly falling short when it comes to leading in the home. The result? Pressure, feelings of failure, shame, and even resignation.

Men naturally want to do things they excel at. So if you tell your husband he's not good at being a leader—or you somehow communicate that through the way you treat him—then he may very well shrink from the task altogether.

I mentioned in chapter 1 that Hugh is a great football player, yet he hesitates to play basketball or even softball at times. If he's not good at something, then he'd rather sit it out. And that is a typically male response. So if your husband knows he's not stellar at being the spiritual leader he needs to be, don't you think he might avoid that role altogether? Wouldn't he prefer to be out from under the scrutiny?

Interestingly, even though Hugh is a pastor, he still struggles at times with feelings of inadequacy—because he is human, because his wife might give him a look that says *What were you thinking?* and because "all have sinned and fall short of the glory of God" (Romans 3:23).

As I consider all the pressure a man faces in this area, I realize that I wouldn't want to have to live under the weight of such a responsibility. It makes me appreciate all the more what Hugh is faced with. I know that eventually I will have to give an account to God for how I teach His Word, how I instruct and disciple women, and how I have taken part in raising my daughter. But if the whole spiritual condition of my home were my responsibility? Lord, help me. And that must be what my husband—and yours—feels at home, constantly.

Because my husband is a pastor, he already bears the weight of the spiritual condition of his congregation on his shoulders. How much more the weight of his own family? And how much more an added weight if I remind, chide, criticize, or instruct him about what he *should* be doing as the spiritual leader in our home? Your husband might be a supervisor, manager, department head, vice president, or even a CEO whose decisions directly affect the well-being of many employees or an entire company. If that's the case, your husband already bears a significant weight of responsibility as a leader. And he needs to know you believe in his ability to lead you and your family too.

Now, perhaps your husband *is* leading, but not in the way you have envisioned for him to do so. (We will talk about that more in the next chapter.) Give your husband a break when it comes to meeting your expectations. And give him a break when it comes to being the spiritual head of the household. I'm not saying you are to dismiss him from that responsibility (only God can do that). Rather, I'm saying lighten up (and I say that with a smile). Find ways to encourage your husband. Help him without trying to do it for him. He would like to be able to lead. It just might be difficult, and that would be true for any of us. For now, it's time to hand him the reins and come alongside him as a partner.

Handing Him the Reins

So how can you partner with your husband and let him lead in the way God designed him to? Provide input—graciously. Pray for him—continually. And praise his ability to lead—even if you don't agree with *how* he leads.

Provide Input—Graciously

Your input is valuable to your husband, but how you provide that input makes all the difference in the world. I have, in the past, made my husband believe that I was so sure of my opinion that I had already decided how we should handle a situation and I was merely running it by him for his agreement with me that I had figured out our dilemma. Not a wise thing to do. I have since learned to look at a situation, ask him for his opinion, and then discuss with him what we should do. I have found that his suggested approach is often a perfectly suitable solution. Perhaps it's not a solution I would have proposed, but what counts is that the matter is resolved amicably. (See why I needed to learn how to inspire my husband so I could eventually write about it? God needed to do some work in *me!*)

Pray for Him—Continually

"Sometimes I don't have all the answers and I feel incapable of leading," Jeff said. But his wife of 24 years always encourages them to pray together about major decisions. "And I know she prays for me too. That's tremendously helpful."

Your husband wants to know you are in his corner. If you, like Alice, can't say, "I'm on board with you" and really mean it, then pray for a submissive spirit that enables you to say, "Because you're my husband, I will honor your decision." And then keep praying for him—and his decision—every step of the way.

Praise Him—Unconditionally

The man in your husband will want to continue to do what he feels he is doing well. Yes, there may be times he doesn't lead effectively. But find something you can praise, such as his initiative. His courage in taking a step. His desire to do what is best. As he steps out and leads, he needs to know the two of you are a team.

My husband recently sent me a text that convinced me his heart wants the best for both of us, and he needed to hear that I still believed in him to lead our family. His text simply said, "I need to know it's you and me forever and through whatever."

My simple response was. "Of course it's forever and through whatever. I promised before. And I'll promise it again."

Hugh seemed like a more confident man, husband, and leader that evening. Or maybe it was just how I perceived him after I gained another glimpse of his heart.

ᦥ From His Perspective ᦥ

He Led, She Led, and Now They Partner Together

Greg, now age 47, is a commander in the Navy. So, naturally he is a capable leader. His wife, Donna, is a mother, entrepreneur, business owner, and quite a leader herself. In some homes, a union between two extremely capable and self-motivated leaders would cause friction. But Greg and Donna have learned to work together as partners.

"My career and her ambition—and her ability to lead—dovetail together perfectly because I spend a lot of time away from home as a Navy officer," Greg said.

Because of Greg's several deployments over the course of their 21-year marriage, Donna has learned to adjust to being the sole leader when her husband is gone and the co-leader when he's home. And that has given Greg a tremendous amount of peace while he is serving his country and trying to stay focused on the job.

"My wife has a lot of inner strength," Greg said. "I've seen a lot of other military personnel whose wives don't handle the separation well—the wife isn't doing well coping with the kids and the finances and paying the bills. Donna is always very good at picking up everything and taking care of it so I can focus on my mission."

For Greg, having a wife who knows how to lead his home is a great source of encouragement to him. "She encourages me most by letting me know that she has things under control at home (as much as she can) so I don't have to worry. Also she displays the strength that a Navy wife must have to endure numerous deployments and lengthy periods of family separation. Upon my return, I never find any surprises. Donna has already handled the things that were in her control, and whatever else needed attention, we would pray about. All was well."

And because Donna owns her own business and has much going on outside her home, she is more than willing to let Greg step back in and lead when he returns.

Greg admits there are some challenges when a man wants his wife to lead in his absence but then wants to resume his role again when he returns, especially when it comes to their finances.

"I have to turn all of the finances over to Donna when I deploy. She has to know everything about what's going on just in case I don't come home. However, I usually resume my role over managing the finances when I return. Sometimes Donna has been reluctant to relinquish the finances to me when I return because she has developed a pretty good system while I was away. But, I'm the one who went to Financial Peace University!"[23]

Donna admits it's challenging to lead for about a year and then turn the reins back over to Greg. It's also difficult for their two young sons to begin looking to dad again for a decision or a need, instead of just mom. It's been difficult, too, for Donna to not assume the "head of the household" role before Greg actually leaves. She will start operating as if he isn't there (in order to adjust to her pending role as leader again), and Greg sees that as her distancing herself from him just before he goes overseas again.

That was how it worked when they were separated by Greg's deployments. And they made the best of it. And now that Greg is no longer being deployed, they have transitioned into a partnership they both find rewarding.

"Now when a decision has to be made, we talk about it," Greg said. "Our marriage is a partnership. We each bring our different perspectives to a situation. For us to make a good decision, we both need input from the other person. I wouldn't make a big decision without talking to Donna and getting her input, and she's pretty much the same. That speaks to the respect we have for each other in the relationship.

"If I were to unexpectedly show up in the driveway with a brand new car, she'd say, 'Well that's nice, but shouldn't we have talked about this?' And it works the same way with her too. That's how we respect one another."

Greg said having a wife with leadership ability has its advantages. "She has a lot of ambition and inner strength. She's not a needy type of person. She has goals and is self-motivated, so she's not just standing at the door waiting for me to come home every day. And best of all," he said, "she's not clingy. She's not insecure. She's not needy."

᧒ Honoring Your Husband's Lead ᧒

Now it's time to put it into practice by completing the following exercise.

1. Express to your husband that you want to be his helper in every sense of the word, but you also want to let him lead in the way he sees best. Ask him about how you can best let him lead in the home. (Be careful not to ask in a way that implies he doesn't lead, but in a way that conveys you realize you may be doing more than he actually wants you to.)

2. Now write out his response or suggestions here.

3. Based on your husband's response, write a prayer in the space below, asking God to help you honor your husband in the ways he mentioned.

A Prayer for You and Your Husband

Teach Me to Let Go

Lord, You are the One who is truly in control of all that happens in our lives. So help me to trust You, first, and then my husband, whom You have put in authority over me. Help me to realize that as I am being obedient to You by coming under his leadership, You will not make me suffer for it. Humble my heart during the times when I feel I do things better than my husband. Help me to honor him by eagerly following his lead. And on the days when I am not truly on board with him, give me a heart of surrender that says, "Not my will, but yours, and I will trust you because you are my husband." Graciously guide us, Lord Jesus, and give my husband the wisdom and strength to be the leader You have designed him to be.

"If you are a wife, you must put your husband first. Even if he opposes our message, you will win him over by what you do. No one else will have to say anything to him, because he will see how you honor God and live a pure life."

1 PETER 3:1-2 CEV

CHAPTER 9

Accepting Him Spiritually

Serena sat across the table from me, understandably frustrated.

"I wish my husband would show more of a hunger for God," she told me. "Back when we met, he was the one who was spiritually strong. I was attracted to him by how involved he was in church and by all the notes that I saw he'd written in his Bible. Now it's like pulling teeth to get him to talk to me about spiritual things. I wish I knew what was going on with him and where he is with God."

We all have visions of what we want our husband to look like spiritually. I know some wives who say, "My husband is everything I've wanted in a man spiritually. He has a thriving relationship with Christ and he's the one who's leading me and our family spiritually."

But I also know many women don't feel that way.

Chances are you are among those who would like your husband to show a little more initiative when it comes to leading your family spiritually. Or maybe you'd like to see more evidence of—or excitement in—your husband's walk with Christ. Or maybe you'd just like to see him have a relationship with Christ in the first place.

If any of those are true in your marriage, then this chapter is for you.

And it's important that we begin by recognizing that, no matter what your hopes and dreams for your husband from a spiritual standpoint, what happens in his relationship with God (or lack of one) comes down to him and God—period.

There's a reason Scripture exhorts women married to unbelievers to "be submissive to your own husbands so that even if any of them are disobedient to the word, they may be won without a word by the behavior of their wives, as they observe your chaste and respectful behavior" (1 Peter 3:1-2 NASB).

Let's look at that same verse in a few other translations:

> You wives must accept the authority of your husbands. Then, even if some refuse to obey the Good News, your godly lives will speak to them without any words. They will be won over by observing your pure and reverent lives (NLT).

> If you are a wife, you must put your husband first. Even if he opposes our message, you will win him over by what you do. No one else will have to say anything to him, because he will see how you honor God and live a pure life (CEV).

> Be good wives to your husband, responsive to their needs. There are husbands who, indifferent as they are to any words about God, will be captivated by your life of holy beauty (MSG).

I often wonder if this Bible passage is particularly intended for us today because God knew just how much women would try to push and pull, hint and convict, and even at times try to manipulate their husbands into sharing their faith or meeting them at the same level in their spiritual walk with the Lord.

I've talked to hundreds of wives over the past 20 years of my teaching ministry, and they have attested to the fact that their words are rarely effective when it comes to trying to convince their unbelieving husbands to submit to God. And even the wives of men who are Christians find themselves at a loss when it comes to trying to get their husbands to develop a deeper relationship with God or to be more committed to the church or spiritual matters.

My friend Theresa told me that she tried for several years to get her husband to be the kind of godly man and spiritual leader that she had envisioned he would be when they got married. She would drop hints, recount great sermons to him, buy books for him on how to be a godly man, and sign him up for every "spiritual" opportunity for men at her church. But her actions made her husband feel as though he couldn't measure up to her heavy load of expectations.

Theresa said, "The best gift I can give my husband is to allow him to be who God created him to be. I have to allow him to grow in his faith on his own. Because when I tried to change him spiritually, I almost ruined our marriage. The only expectations our husbands are to live up to are the Lord's."

Well said, Theresa.

Now there are ways we can encourage our husbands to grow spiritually. What do they look like?

They *don't* look like pulling, pushing, or manipulating. In fact, they usually have to do with backing off and letting your husband pursue his walk with God *without* your help.

Now please don't think I'm being critical because I don't understand what it's like to live with an unbeliever or a man who isn't on the same page as you spiritually. I do understand your situation if you are desperate to see your husband be the godly man he is called to be. Over the last 20 years, Hugh and I have seen many well-intentioned wives trying to pull their husbands along spiritually. We value the wife's good intentions—of course she wants her man to live for God and grow spiritually. And kudos to her for pursuing her spiritual growth without his push behind her. But we women, in general, tend to be impatient when it comes to the spiritual growth of our men.

Coming on Too Strong

Many of us women want our husbands to look and act like the "spiritual Ken dolls" we imagined we would one day marry. But we have to realize we are not "spiritual Barbie" and therefore our husbands can't be spiritual Ken.

According to Hugh, men would much rather be spiritual GI Joe. Hugh has told me, "I'd much rather have a scar on my face from battling the enemy and be carrying weapons over my shoulder for the spiritual warfare that is in front of me than be neat and clean, decked out in a coordinating outfit, and carrying a high-fashion European shoulder bag!"

All of that to say, your husband's idea of spirituality may look very different than yours. Just because he views church or the Christian life in a different way than you doesn't mean he lacks a personal desire for God to transform his life. And he might not feel as comfortable as you do about sitting in a circle with other couples and sharing about his marital struggles at a weekly Bible study group, but that doesn't mean he's not praying for you and your marriage.

Back in chapter 1, we noted that one of the differences between women and men, generally speaking, is that women prefer interdependency, collaboration, coordination, and cooperation, whereas men tend toward independence and autonomy. Another difference is that women tend to be more open about sharing their problems with others, while men tend to keep their concerns to themselves.

Now think about those two differences alone and what they might mean in terms of what you are seeing—or not seeing—in your man's spiritual life. They might explain why you are not hearing a lot about his experiences with God, what he is reading or not reading in the Word, and how he might or might not desire to grow spiritually.

Relational vs. Functional

I asked my girlfriends to tell me of the highlights of their faith and pursuit of God, and here are the answers they gave me:

- "I play worship CDs in my car on my commute to work and that helps keep me focused on the Lord. In this way, I am able to invite Jesus into my day while I am on my way to work!"

- "I've been waking up every morning and saying, 'Good morning, Jesus. How would You have me serve You today?'"

- "I love seeing how God orchestrates the conversations and events in my life, especially after I've made it a point of spending time with Him."

- "Going on prayer walks helps me stay focused on God."

- "I'm reading everything there is in the Bible about God's love and asking myself how life would be different if I really believed and applied those truths."

- "I have been so touched at the gentle ways God has been pursuing me and showing me He loves me and will provide for me."

Then I asked my husband and a few spiritual (and seemingly unspiritual) men to tell me what they consider the highlights of their faith and pursuit of God. Here is how *they* answered:

- "I'm learning some awesome things about how the early church Fathers related to Christ."

- "I'm discovering new truths in the Word of God daily, and I'm writing them down and thinking about them throughout the day."

- "I'm re-evaluating my eschatological beliefs in light of the parallels I'm seeing in the Old and New Testaments that I never knew were there, and it's making me re-examine the person of Jesus, how I see the kingdom of God, and the peace I now have as a believer."

- "The Bible continues to amaze me with how relevant it is in my life, job, and family."

Did you catch some key differences? The women's answers were highly relational and experiential. They tended to talk about the *relationship* they have with Christ and how it makes them *feel*. By contrast, the men's answers were more functional. They talked about what they were learning and discovering as a result of study. Same God, same desires to grow. Different personalities, different approaches.

One man told me, "I had a stoplight moment during one of our small-group prayer sessions. I was trying to stay focused on prayer and my young son kept wiggling, whispering, and trying to get my attention, and I kept trying to quiet him down. Then I looked at him and noticed how he is growing quickly right in front of my eyes. And I saw myself in him. Here I am, trying to quiet him down so I can focus on prayer, and all this time God has been trying to get *my* attention and quiet *me* down so that I will listen to *Him*."

I don't know that I've ever heard a woman tell me something like that. Deep insights *do* come from men. You just might not be seeing them, or hearing about them from your husband.

Just because your man isn't expressive about his faith doesn't mean it isn't as real or deep. It's just expressed differently.

Your Silent Witness

Charles Swindoll, a former pastor and the author of numerous books, says, "We men are far more closed—closed toward God and closed toward one another. But women have an openness, a warmth, a responsiveness to the things of God. Women have a desire to grow, to react, to feel, to show affection toward the things of God that is not found in the average man."[24] At least, it isn't often *expressed* by the average man.

I share Swindoll's quote with you to help you see the importance of having girlfriends in your life with whom you can relate on a spiritual and female level. Because chances are, your husband may not be expressing an interest in spiritual matters in the way you want or need him to. And that's especially true if your husband is not a Christian. But that's okay, because Scripture commands you to show God to him through your reverent behavior rather than through your words.

Because this chapter is about "accepting" your husband's spirituality—or lack of it—I want to let you know how you can accept your husband for who he is so that God can do the work in and through him that you were not intended to accomplish. And hopefully you will experience relief from a burden you were never meant to carry. God never made it your responsibility to bring your spouse along spiritually. In fact, one of the best things you might be able to do is simply get out of the way.

Earlier in this chapter we read that wives of unbelieving husbands should be submissive to their husbands "*so that* even if any of them are disobedient to the word, they may be won without a word by the behavior of their wives, as they observe [their] chaste and respectful behavior" (1 Peter 3:1 NASB). Note the three main points of action in those verses: submission, purity, and reverence.

Then the next two verses add this:

> Don't depend on things like fancy hairdos or gold jewelry or expensive clothes to make you look beautiful. Be beautiful in your heart by being gentle and quiet. This kind of beauty will last, and God considers it very special (verses 3-4 CEV).

So what is this *reverent behavior* that will win over our husbands spiritually? What is this inner beauty and "hidden person of the heart" that Scripture says will have a profound impact on our husbands, drawing them to a relationship with Christ? It's speaking of character—a character of faith that says more through our actions than our words. Now, while 1 Peter 3:1-4 is talking about a woman's behavior in the eyes of an unbelieving husband, I want to add that the same kind of reverent behavior is very winsome in the eyes of a Christian man too.

What if you were to be so lost in God that your husband had to seek Him in order to find you?

That's what I want my life to look like! On the days that my husband doesn't understand me, I want him to think *not* that I'm too hormonal or that I'm too stressed, but that I'm so in love with God that he needs to go to the Lord and say, "Show me the depth and mysteries of this woman I married so I can connect with her in a way that pleases You."

I believe you want that too.

Living It Out

I talked to a friend in ministry who counsels couples, and she told me that wives have a habit of telling their husbands to trust God, but they don't exhibit such trust in their own lives.

"A woman came to me recently and asked for help because her husband had lost his job and had subsequently been deeply depressed," my friend told me. "She said she had been telling her husband to just trust God, but he continued to worry." So my counselor friend asked this woman, "Are *you* trusting God by your words and actions every day?"

"What do you mean?" the woman asked.

"Exactly!" said my friend. "Instead of *telling* your husband to trust God, *show* him by your life what it means to trust God. Instead of reminding him that God will provide, live as if He is already providing." Your "encouragement" to your husband is not true encouragement—which literally means to "put courage into"—until you are demonstrating that kind of courage and faith in your own life.

With this in mind, let's look at some ways we can have an effect upon our husbands' spirituality.

Be a Woman of Purity

Why would Scripture point out that the "purity and reverence of your lives" can win your husband over to the Lord? Because purity makes you stand apart from the rest of the world. Being pure in thought, speech, and action shows your sanctification and God's touch on your life. If your husband is not a believer, or you have a husband who isn't as committed to Christ as you believe he should be, look at your own commitment level and ask yourself: Does everyone who encounters me know, beyond a doubt, that I am separated from this world because of my love and obedience to Christ? Can my husband see that plainly in my life?

One way we can be pure—and separated from the rest of the world—is to not have a critical or argumentative spirit. Philippians 2:14-15 says:

> Do everything without grumbling or arguing, so that you
> may become blameless and pure, "children of God without
> fault in a warped and crooked generation." Then you will
> shine among them like stars in the sky.

That passage basically says you will stand out from the crowd when you don't complain or argue. Do you know what it's like to be around a person who is constantly pleasant and grateful, someone who always sees the glass as half-full rather than half-empty? It's refreshing, isn't it? Scripture calls *you* to be that kind of person in your husband's presence, and it will change him for the better. In another translation, Philippians 2:15 says a person who does all things without grumbling or complaining will "appear as lights in the world."[25]

Jesus told his followers: "Let your light shine before others, that they may see your good deeds and glorify your Father in heaven" (Matthew 5:16). So shine, woman of God—by being grateful and gracious—so that others (including your husband) will see your good deeds and glorify your Father in heaven!

Be a Woman of Reverence

Reverence is another character quality that can help win our husbands over without a word from us. To revere your husband is to respect or admire him *even when you don't agree with what he says or does.* Any woman will gladly obey and respect her husband when she knows he is absolutely right in the decisions he makes and how he leads. But what if your husband struggles when it comes to making decisions or leading? And chances are, if he doesn't know or live for Christ, he may struggle in many areas of his life. How much more, then, are you ministering to his heart when you respect and admire him out of a love for God and a desire to please your heavenly Father first?

Gwen, a fairly new believer who is married to an unbeliever, has come to realize the more she grows in obedience to and love for her Lord, the more difficult it is to continue to respect her husband, especially when he holds different values than she does and is not letting

God deal with sin issues in his life. But out of a desire to remain obedient to God, she prays for wisdom and discernment to know specifically how she can serve as a helper to her husband. She realizes that giving him respect—simply because he is her husband—is pleasing to God. And therefore she offers that to her husband as an offering to the Lord.

Be a Woman of Gentleness

Proverbs 15:1 says, "A gentle answer turns away wrath, but a harsh word stirs up anger." The opposite of gentleness is roughness, callousness, harshness. Husbands are attracted to the softness in their wives—their ability to smooth over a situation, say a kind word at the appropriate time, hold a crying baby and calm him or her down. Does your husband see those same qualities of gentleness expressed in how you relate to *him?* When I try to offer a constructive suggestion to my husband about how he leads our family, it *always* goes over better when I offer it with gentleness.

Be a Woman with a Quiet Spirit

A woman with a gentle and quiet spirit is not a cantankerous woman, or a disgraceful or foolish woman, as is described in the book of Proverbs.[26] This woman is calm, not worried; quiet, not stressed. She is quietly trusting in her God to come through in ways that perhaps her husband cannot comprehend. A quiet spirit says, without words,

- "I'm trusting God through this."
- "I'm praying about this and putting my faith to work."
- "I'm not going to worry about this situation because I know God is in control."

Having a quiet spirit means we don't stress about a situation we can't control. (And that quietness may convey to your husband that you're actually trusting *him* too!) Having a quiet spirit means not having to talk through everything with your husband, but taking matters to the Lord and discussing them with Him. When you do that, you can receive the peace God gives when you choose to not worry about anything, but instead, "pray about everything," telling God what you need and thanking Him for all He has done. Scripture says, "Pray about everything. Tell God what you need, and thank him for all he has done. Then you will experience God's peace, which exceeds anything we can understand. His peace will guard your hearts and minds as you live in Christ Jesus" (Philippians 4:6-7 NLT).

And how can we cultivate this quiet spirit? We find the answer in the next verse: Focus your mind on "whatever is true, whatever is noble, whatever is right, whatever is pure, whatever is lovely, whatever is admirable—if anything is excellent or praiseworthy—think about such things" (Philippians 4:8-9).

The alternative is to focus on all the "what ifs" in life. Those are the things that make us women with an anxious spirit—not women who have a quiet spirit "of great worth in God's sight" (1 Peter 3:4).

✑ From His Perspective ✐

I asked Hugh to give some pastoral advice to a wife who feels her husband is not where she'd like him to be spiritually. And this was his counsel:

If your husband doesn't seem interested in spiritual matters, it could be that his masculine spirit is having trouble resonating with the particular church services you are both attending. Research has shown that the primary worship services of many churches tend to reflect more of what women respond and relate to than men. As a pastor, I am always evaluating our church's services to be sure that men, as well as women, can engage with what is transpiring. Let's be honest—a lot of men have trouble eagerly singing songs to a masculine God and Savior in which they have to say, "Lord, You're beautiful" or "Jesus, hold me close." Now that may feel like a point of frustration for you because you're probably not in a position to alter the way your church does its worship services. But this may help shed light on perhaps why your husband seems to have checked out at church.

I've had the opportunity to see men up close and personal come alive and grow spiritually, so I know that in the right environment, it is possible for that to happen. I've led two separate small focus groups of men through a year-long study of *Wild at Heart* by John Eldredge. Yes, you heard that right—some men devoted to growing spiritually once a week for an entire year. One man had never prayed out loud in front of other people, but after a couple of months he was one of the first guys to pray when it came to that part of our study. On the final night of this study with the second group, we didn't want it to end. In fact, one man said, "Do we have to stop?" And another guy asked, "What should we do next?"

Start by simply asking your husband what motivates him when it comes to church and spiritual things. Maybe he is willing to consider going to a men's retreat or finding a Bible study for men. Ask him if he finds church boring, irrelevant, or unchallenging, and talk about what adjustments can be made there. Or, perhaps your husband's schedule would make it easier for him to attend a Saturday evening church service rather than one on Sunday morning.

It's important that you not make your husband feel that he has to "report to you" about the status of his spirituality, or that you are doing a performance review of this area of his life. Ask him honest questions, and be willing to accept his honest answers. Always be encouraging. If your husband is more of a cognitive learner, buy him a book or CD on spiritual issues. If he tends to be more of a hands-on type of learner, see if there are any church projects in which he can work side-by-side with other men. In such cases, I guarantee you that more than just physical labor will take place. Your husband will end up having conversations with other men that will open the door for some real soul work to take place. And hopefully your husband will see that Christian men can still be men.

If your husband is not a believer, your first call of duty is to pray for his salvation. That is a work neither you nor anyone else can accomplish in his life—his salvation is 100 percent a work of the Holy Spirit. So pray that God would open his heart and mind to his need for Christ. And be sure you are living your Christian life in a manner that honors the Lord and makes Him worthy of your husband's attention, and a force your husband must reckon with.

❧ Letting Him Go ❧

You can experience peace and relief as a wife by surrendering your husband's spirituality into God's hands. As you pray for him—rather than prod him—you can be confident God will do the work that you cannot.

Here are some more ways to let go of your expectations on him and let God do the work:

1. In the space below, list ways that God might be working in your husband's life that might not appear spiritual but may be God's blessings, nonetheless. For example, is he doing well in his job? Does he have good relationships with his children, or his co-workers? Is he seen as a man of honesty and integrity? Thank God for each one as you list them here.

2. You can shine in your reverent and pure lifestyle and be a spiritual inspiration to your husband by living out the fruit of the Spirit listed in Galatians 5:22-23. Pick three "fruit" from that passage, list them below, and next to each one write a simple, practical way you can display that characteristic to your husband in your everyday life (I did the first one for you):

    a. Joy: I will have a positive attitude when I see and talk
       to my husband today, with the intention that he sees
       in me the joy of the Lord.

    b. _____ :

    c. _____ :

    d. _____ :

⌒ A Prayer for Your Husband's Spiritual Life ∽

Lord, Draw Him to Your Heart

Lord, thank You that You are in pursuit of my husband's
heart just as much as You've been in pursuit of mine. And
You know, far better than me, the depths of his relationship
with You, how to reach him and take him further, and how
to light a fire of passion within him for You alone.

    Forgive me for the times I've tried to manipulate him
into doing things my way. Please see that my heart truly
wants to be one with him spiritually. And please show me
the times I am getting in the way of that. Forgive me, too,
for the times I've tried to pull him along spiritually, believing I could somehow sway or encourage him toward a
deeper faith. Only Your convicting Holy Spirit can work in

hearts and transform nonbelievers into believers and believers into committed disciples.

Help me, Lord, to look to You for my own spiritual growth and to pray constantly for my husband. And help me to remember that Your Word says You will complete the work You have begun in my husband (Philippians 1:6).

> *"Let's not just talk about love;*
> *let's practice real love."*
>
> 1 John 3:18 MSG

CHAPTER 10

Loving Him as God Does

I received an e-mail from a reader just this morning as I was sitting down to write this last chapter on how to love our husbands. She had discovered some disturbing news about her husband. And her words sounded desperate, if not battle-weary.

She said hers was "a marriage filled with stress, conflict, disrespect, and verbal abuse for 25 years," and she had just discovered something else about him that set her over the edge. He was repentant and promised to change, but she was hesitant to take him back. Her question was this: "Would a woman be wrong if she just couldn't remain married to this man, even if her children say they want her to forgive him and keep the family together?"

In the Bible, I am aware of only two situations in which leaving one's marriage partner is permissible: (1) when a spouse has been sexually unfaithful; and (2) when an unbelieving spouse chooses not to live any longer with a believer.[27] Yet in today's society we have added more "reasons" to the list: physical, verbal or emotional abuse; alcohol and drug addictions; emotional neglect; and so on. My heart grieves at the situations wives endure today—they want to obey God, yet they struggle over being "trapped" in a loveless, painful, or unfulfilling marriage.

"God, I shouldn't have to write a chapter telling women how to love their husbands," I complained. "The way You designed marriage, that love should just come naturally!"

Yes, God designed marriage to work perfectly. And I imagine before sin came into the picture, Eve had no problem at all loving her perfect, sinless husband. But once she brought sin into the situation—and Eve did sin first—a whole new dynamic fell into place. As a result of sin's presence in our lives, the only kind of "love" that comes naturally is that feeling of infatuation we have when we first fall in love. Back when we first married, we saw in our husbands what we wanted to see. "Love is blind," they say. And then through the years, our eyes were opened to reality and we saw many things we may not have wanted to see at first. We saw that our husbands were sinners. We saw they were capable of letting us down and causing us pain.

But love—God's kind of love—sees all and *still* loves. God knows everything about us, including our imperfections, and He still loves us. He knows what lurks in our minds and hearts, and He knows not only our past sins but our future ones as well—and He still extends love. God loves us unconditionally and in spite of who we really are. And that's how He calls us to love our husbands.

In the New Testament, the apostle Paul urged a young man, Titus, to "teach the older women to be reverent in the way they live... *Then* they can urge the younger women to love their husbands and children" (Titus 2:3-4, emphasis added). Why did the young women need to be *trained* to love their husbands and children? Because true love is not something we *feel*. It's something we are *taught*—by how Christ loves us.

Jesus Himself said in John 13:34, "A new command I give you: Love one another. *As I have loved you,* so you must love one another." That is a pretty tall order. He gave His life for those whom He loves. And to expect us to do the same is pretty radical. But He doesn't expect us to do this in our own power.

Because the Lord is the author and perfecter of love, He is able to love our husbands through us when we feel as if we don't have anything left. And in His grace, He shows us exactly how to do that.

What Makes Men Feel Loved

I asked husbands to tell me what makes them feel loved by their wives in spite of their differences and all they wish they could be, but aren't. Listen to the responses from their hearts:

- "When she accepts me without feeling the need to fundamentally change who I am."

- "When she upholds my character and personality to others and doesn't feel the need to apologize for who I am or explain me to others."

- "When she's always willing to start over."

- "When she can show me she loves me by still being nice to me even when I'm a jerk."

- "When she doesn't compare me to others; she doesn't try to change me."

- "By telling me I am a great husband and father and that she is fully satisfied with who I am today and not who she hopes I can be molded into tomorrow."

- "When she tells me and others that she feels honored that I am her husband, I know that she loves me for who I am."

- "By the way she extends grace to me even when I snap at her and do things that are unattractive."

- "When she loves me in spite of myself, just like God does."

Did you hear the common thread running through those responses? The sound of humility from a man who realizes he is not so easy to love? The gratitude that he is even loved in the first place? The conviction he feels when he does wrong and his wife still remains selfless and loving?

Your husband *does* notice when you love and accept him, even when he's not being so lovable or accepting. Your husband may be tough, but he is also tender on the inside. And if you dig deep enough, you will find in him a heart like yours. Your husband longs to be loved and appreciated for who he is, and wants to be forgiven for the times he blows it.

Chances are you're already loving your husband for who he is and forgiving him when he messes up. I believe that is the kind of woman you are, especially because you have made it this far into a book that is all about how you can minister to his heart. And in this chapter, I want to encourage you to do for your husband what God has done for you—to go beyond the expected to the extravagant. Lavish love on him. And by so doing, you will be lavishing on yourself the blessings of showing Calvary's kind of love.

Showing God's Love for Him

In her book *Helper by Design,* Elyse Fitzpatrick says, "It is right for you to love your husband, even in his rebellion, because God loved you in your rebellion."[28]

If your husband is an unbeliever who blows it every now and then (just like you do), love him as God does. If your husband is a believer who knows better but still blows it at times (just like you do), love him as God does. Love him as you love yourself. But mostly, love him as God loves him.

How does God love him? The same way He loves you—unconditionally and without reservation. God's love for you is such that "neither death nor life, neither angels nor demons, neither the present nor the future, nor any powers, neither height nor depth, nor anything else in all creation, will be able to separate us from the love of God that is in Christ Jesus our Lord" (Romans 8:38-39).

Wow. What if *that* verse were included in our wedding vows? Of course, we don't have the power to uphold that kind of promise to love. Death will one day separate us from our spouse. And if we're not careful, something present or future, something more powerful than ourselves, or possibly even someone else on this earth could very easily separate us from the love we have or intend to have for our spouse. But God is fully able to keep that kind of promise to love us.

You are not God…nor can you, in your own power, love your husband as God does. But through God's power working in you, you can become one who sacrificially loves your husband and shows to him the kind of love Christ has for you—and for him.

Jesus told His disciples in John 15:12, "My command is this: Love each other as I have loved you." And then, in case there was any question about how much Jesus loved them, He clarified His statement by describing the kind of self-sacrificial love He had for them and that He expected them to have for one another: "Greater love has no one than this: to lay down one's life for one's friends. You are my friends if you do what I command" (verses 13-14).

We are to love our husbands the way Jesus Christ loved us. He laid down His life for us; He died on the cross for us.

So how can you love your husband as Christ loves you?

Show Him Sacrificial Love

Over the course of writing this book, God has been taking me through a process of brokenness—brokenness as a woman, a wife, a mother, and as a daughter. Earlier in the year I asked God to show me ways in which I need to be more like Him—ways I need more of Him and less of me.

"God, please break me of pride, self-righteousness, a critical spirit, and other attitudes that hurt You and others," I prayed. And God has shown me much of myself that I didn't necessarily want to see. In His love and grace, He has been showing me who I am—and who I'm capable of being—apart from Him. The picture is humbling, to say the least.

One of the things He showed me is how very easy it is for me to put myself first. It's so natural for me that it's embarrassing. I feel ashamed when I think of my Lord's example of washing His disciples' feet and dying for the sins of mankind. I'm sure my selfishness is displayed in my marriage more than I realize, and that my husband sees it. And of course, that is not Calvary love.

Amy Carmichael, who asked God to make her house empty so that His house could be full, knew self-sacrifice. She gave up marriage so she could serve God as a missionary caring for orphan children in India. And during her lifetime, she wrote up glimpses of what our lack of love looks like compared to the perfect illustration of Calvary love. Here are some examples from her book titled *If*:

> If in dealing with one who does not respond, I weary of the strain and slip from under the burden, then I know nothing of Calvary love.
>
> If I have not the patience of my Saviour with souls who grow slowly; if I know little of travail (a sharp and painful thing) till Christ be fully formed in them, then I know nothing of Calvary love.
>
> If I hold on to choices of any kind, just because they are my choice; if I give any room to my private likes and dislikes, then I know nothing of Calvary love.
>
> If something I am asked to do for another feels burdensome; if, yielding to an inward unwillingness, I avoid doing it, then I know nothing of Calvary love.[29]

How can our husbands not be encouraged, inspired, and motivated when we demonstrate to them Calvary love? The kind of love that sacrifices self for the benefit of others. The kind of love that says, "Not my will, but yours." "Not my happiness, but yours." "Not my preferences, but yours." "Not my fulfillment, but yours."

Yes, God created marriage to be equally fulfilling for both partners. But we are sinners, and therefore at least one of us must bend and become unlike the other. At least one of us must choose to be more like Christ. Because *you* are the one reading this book, we'll assume that one in the marriage will be you.

To show sacrificial love to your husband is to ask yourself, "What is it costing me?" Yes, during the early years of marriage it is a joy to love our husbands. But as the years go by and the pressures of life set in, oftentimes it becomes more of a challenge to show that love consistently. And if that love does not cost you something in some way, it is not sacrificial as Christ's love is for us. Such love will sometimes cost us an inconvenience, a delay, a setback. Other times, sacrificial love will cost us our own desires. But such love is worth it. It shows our husbands—and God—that we know *something* of Calvary love.

Practice Protective Love

Throughout the Bible, God is seen as a loving and protective God. He comes through for His people. He protects His own. Do you have a protective love going on for your husband?

Hugh and I have been in situations where things were said publicly about him that really hurt us. And when that happens I have felt, immediately, a strong surge of protective love. The inner tigress in me wanted to claw at those who said something disrespectful or accusatory. On one occasion I remember fidgeting in my seat and shifting my feet. At one point, I started to jump up in defense of Hugh, but he put his hand on my knee as if to say, "Calm down, it's okay." *He* was comforting *me* as my heart was being ripped out about what was being said about *him*. In those moments, if I could have, I would've taken the brunt of those false allegations myself to spare him that pain. And if that were the case, I *knew* he would never allow such things to be said of me.

My protective love kicks in during those times. And I've often wondered why I don't have that kind of protective love for him *every* day. O God, give me a heart that protects my husband at all costs. Help me to show him love and respect that far outweighs and refills what the people in this world have taken from him.

Chances are your husband is in some kind of arena where he can be "beat up" too. There may be days when your husband is disrespected at his office or workplace, by his grown children, by someone in his extended family. Whether he's a coach, an executive, a supervisor, a teacher, or an employee working under someone else, he has his days, to be sure, when he is the target of accusation, the brunt of jokes, the disappointment of others, the one who let the team down. Those are the days he needs your understanding smile and the reassurance that no matter what anyone else thinks of him, the most important woman in his world still believes he's her hero. That's the kind of protective, reassuring love he needs so he can get back out there and face it all again the next day. Can you more than make up for the hurts and difficulties he faces by giving him more than his share of love, respect, and defending love? I hope so. That kind of love protects his heart when it is broken. It helps assure him that he is still somebody of value in your eyes. You are truly his helper, in all senses of the word, when you show him protective love.

Practice Persevering Love

Scripture speaks frequently of God's great loving-kindness, which lasts forever. His love is an unfailing love.

I believe the most thorough description of love that we can find in Scripture is in 1 Corinthians 13:4-7. Quoted at many weddings, this passage describes enduring love—the kind of love that just won't quit. Here we see a beautiful description of God's love, and we are instructed to practice this love toward others—and that especially includes our husbands:

> Love is patient, love is kind. It does not envy, it does not boast, it is not proud. It does not dishonor others, it is not self-seeking, it is not easily angered, it keeps no record of wrongs. Love does not delight in evil but rejoices with the truth. It *always* protects, *always* trusts, *always* hopes, *always* perseveres (emphasis added).

If that last line didn't convict your heart enough, look at the opening words of the next verse, where we are told more about this love we are to practice: "Love never fails" (verse 8).

Because so many of us are already familiar with that passage of Scripture, I'd like for us to get a fresh look at it by reading it in a more contemporary translation in the hopes it will hit you in places that perhaps it hadn't before:

Love never gives up.
Love cares more for others than for self.
Love doesn't want what it doesn't have.
Love doesn't strut,
Doesn't have a swelled head,
Doesn't force itself on others,
Isn't always "me first,"
Doesn't fly off the handle,
Doesn't keep score of the sins of others,
Doesn't revel when others grovel,
Takes pleasure in the flowering of truth,
Puts up with anything,
Trusts God always,
Always looks for the best,
Never looks back,
But keeps going to the end.[30]

My husband and I were talking the other day about the fact that far fewer marriages would be struggling today if just *one* partner in every marriage practiced that definition of love. Now, can you imagine what that marriage would be like if *both* partners practiced enduring love? There would be no strife, no stress, no bitterness, no built-up baggage. There would be no devastation or divorce. There would be two people who daily give up their rights to themselves so they can serve one another. There would be a perfect picture, in our love toward each other, of God's love toward us.

Maybe your husband doesn't seem like the man he once was. Yet you are still with him. That is persevering love. That is love that says, "I made a promise; now I'm keeping it." God did the same with you and me. Take a look at His never-failing, unending, persevering love for *you*:

He has promised He will never leave you.

> Never will I leave you; never will I forsake you (Hebrews 13:5).

Can you say this to your husband and truly mean it as God means it toward you?

He is always thinking only the best about you.

> How precious to me are your thoughts, God! How vast is the sum of them! Were I to count them, they would outnumber the grains of sand (Psalm 139:17-18).

Can you say that your mind is always filled with good thoughts about your husband?

He is gentle toward you when you're broken.

> He heals the brokenhearted and binds up their wounds (Psalm 147:3).

Are you gentle toward your husband even when he is angry or unlovable, which is how he might respond when he's hurt?

He promises nothing will ever come between the two of you.

> [Nothing] will be able to separate us from the love of God (Romans 8:39).

Are you clinging to any conditions or exceptions in your mind when it comes to loving your husband? Is there something that he could do that would end it for the two of you? God holds no such reservations about you. He has promised that absolutely *nothing*—and that includes anything you could do—will ever come between the two of you. *That* is persevering love.

He loved you so much He was willing to die for you so you could be together for eternity.

> God so loved the world that he gave his one and only Son, that whoever believes in him shall not perish but have eternal life (John 3:16).

I once heard it said, "Don't marry someone you believe you can live with. Marry someone you know you can't live without." Have you cemented your love for your husband so deeply that you are convinced you would never want to separate from him? In a sense, that's how God felt toward you. He sacrificed His Son so that the two of you would never have to be separated.

He loved you in spite of yourself, and still does.

> God demonstrates his own love for us in this: While we were still sinners, Christ died for us (Romans 5:8).

Are you willing to show sacrificial love to your husband even when he doesn't deserve it? Even when he has his back turned toward you? That's the kind of love God showed to us. Even when we were at our worst as sinners, He died for us.

Scripture tells us:

> This is the kind of love we are talking about—not that we once upon a time loved God, but that he loved us and sent his Son as a sacrifice to clear away our sins and the damage they've done to our relationship with God. My dear, dear friends, if God loved us like this, we certainly ought to love each other.[31]

Based on God's ever-persevering love for you, you are to love your husband…

> even when he's annoying you
> even when he's inconsiderate
> even when he's clearly "unlovable"
> even when he's clearly wrong and unrepentant

Extend Renewing Love

Because we are not like God, who never grows weary or wounded, we must know how to renew our love for our husbands. We can't simply wait around for our feelings to be there. I'm so glad God's love for us isn't based on His feelings! Rather, He has *determined* to love us, regardless. We must love our husbands that way too. Because the world will take it out of us. Pain will take it out of us. The everyday stuff of life will take it out of us. But thanks be to God, He can replenish it in us.

In Isaiah 40:28-31 we have this encouragement from God, who can fill you up with love for your husband:

> Do you not know? Have you not heard? The LORD is the everlasting God, the Creator of the ends of the earth. He will not grow tired or weary, and his understanding no one can fathom. He gives strength to the weary and increases the power of the weak. Even youths grow tired and weary, and young men stumble and fall; but those who hope in the LORD will renew their strength. They will soar on wings like eagles; they will run and not grow weary, they will walk and not be faint.

If your love for your husband has waned, how do you renew it? How do you get back that delight in him when he—or something in this life—has taken it out of you? By waiting on the Lord for His strength, which will enable you to love your husband, and by going back to what first drew the two of you together.

Sometimes the easiest way to fall back in love with your man is to remember what first brought you together. I asked several wives—all of whom have been married at least 10 years—to tell me what made them fall in love with their husbands. When they answered their eyes lit up, and here is what they said:

- "I fell in love with him because of his calm, peaceful, and cheerful personality."

- "He is steady, godly and predictable in his character. I love that and always will."

- "He is a very gentle, loving man of integrity."

- "He is honest, sometimes painfully so, but can be trusted

because of that. He is loyal and committed and puts his family first as much as possible."

- "He is a typical East Coast prep school conservative guy who loves learning and teaching, but underneath he is a kid from New Jersey who loves sports and the togetherness of family."

- "He was and is *so* funny. He makes me laugh so hard!"

- "His faith is strong, and that is very attractive. He's a great spiritual leader."

- "He is humble. He's great about conflict resolution."

- "I fell in love with the person that he is. I love his integrity and intelligence. I love that he has ambition and works hard. I like that he is down to earth and not showy."

- "He's the most honest man I know. Even though there have been times when I have wanted him to tell me what *I* wanted to hear, I've learned to appreciate his honesty!"

- "He appears very professional. He's neat, organized, and detail-oriented. And he loves to hunt and fish. Before I met my husband, I stereotyped the 'outdoorsy' guys as being more rugged and less professional. Somehow my husband is *both!*"

- "I love the fact he's very thorough. He thinks before he speaks and is eloquent. He had a habit of writing the sweetest things to me. He is also firmly dedicated to me and our family. He is a wonderful father and he adores his grandchildren. I really love that about him."

Now, if I had asked those wives what they *don't* like about their husbands, I'm sure they could have listed quite a few things. But getting them to focus on the character qualities and traits that first drew them to their husbands ignited a spark in their hearts that showed in their eyes. So when you find it hard to love your husband, think back upon what drew you to him in the beginning…and let that help you renew your love!

Renewing Your Love for Your Husband

Take some time now to think about and list the qualities you found attractive in your husband when you first started dating or got married:

In light of what you wrote above, combined with what you know and admire about your husband now, how would you say you two complement each other? (Think in terms of his strengths and your weaknesses; as well as your strengths and his weaknesses.) Write out your thoughts here:

Now, at dinner tonight, or sometime when your husband is relaxed, bless him by sharing your list with him. You might conclude by saying, "And these are the same reasons I still love you today."

But before you do that, won't you bring your list to the Lord and praise Him for the unique man He gave to you in marriage? I hope so. And as you do, God will give you *His* heart for your husband.

✑ From His Perspective ✑

"She shows her love for me through her forgiveness."

My brother, Dan—who has been married 20 years and has one of the most peaceful, blessed, and joyful marriages I've seen—told me this about how love works between him and his wife, Debbie:

"The best way my wife shows her love for me is through her forgiveness. After we've had an argument, I feel like a complete heel and I don't even love myself at that point. And that's when she forgives me and shows me Christ's love for me.

"It's when I realize I don't deserve such love that her love becomes so much more meaningful. There are times I want to cling to my hurts; I want to throw them back in her face. Yet in the course of wanting to do those things, I come to realize how evil my heart can be. And that's when I get down on myself because I see how evil I am. But then my wife comes along and forgives me, and redeems the whole situation. And that brings me back to Christ and what He did for me.

"Her forgiveness of me takes away any excuse I have to not forgive her. It's when I see Christ in Debbie that I get convicted about what I did to need forgiveness in the first place. Her forgiveness shows me Christ's forgiveness for me and convicts me at a deeper level than just what I did to make her upset. I come face-to-face with how I've wounded Christ.

"The Holy Spirit convicts me even when my wife commits an offense and hasn't asked for forgiveness. Instead of forcing her to acknowledge what she did, I would come to realize I needed to forgive her no matter what. We are to forgive not because someone apologizes and asks for forgiveness, but because Christ forgave us."

Putting Love to the Test

In 1 John 3:18 we are told, "Let's not just talk about love; let's practice real love" (MSG). My prayer is that you won't merely read those words, but that you'll take them to heart and apply them to your life. As you close out this chapter thinking of what first drew you to your husband and what you know of him today, and how much complete acceptance and forgiveness means to a man, I hope you will take this opportunity to commit yourself to him anew. And the reason this is not a "take your husband by the hand and pray this prayer together" type of assignment is because this commitment starts—and ends—with you. You are the one who had the heart to pick up this book and learn what you could do to bless your husband's life. So now, taking what you've learned, commit your heart and life to your husband all over again. And I'm right there with you in doing the same!

⚘ Practicing God's Kind of Love ⚘

1. What are some ways you can serve your husband this week to show him sacrificial love? (Think in terms of putting your needs, desires, or schedule aside in order to serve him.)

2. How can you practice protective love for your husband . . .

in your conversations with others?

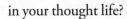

in your thought life?

in your day-to-day routine?

3. Determine to show persevering love to your husband today by incorporating one (or more) of the following (you may wish to write in a few additional ones of your own):

- I will not react to a comment from my husband that rubs me the wrong way, but will choose to give him the benefit of the doubt (1 Corinthians 13:4-7).

- I will find something about my husband to praise God for, regardless of anything he might say or do today.

- I will find a fruit of the Spirit (listed in Galatians 5:22-23) and practice it specifically toward my husband (yes, that's a reminder to apply what you learned from the last chapter!).

- I will take an aspect of God's love for me that means the most to me and extend it toward my husband today (see pages 169-72 for a reminder of the way God loves you).

ᴄ A Prayer for You and Your Husband ᴄ

Father God, how good of You, in Your wisdom and love, to lay it upon my heart to want to come alongside, uplift, encourage, and inspire my husband—for Your glory, as well as the benefit to my husband's soul. May You see in my heart a desire to have a marriage that pleases You in all respects. You have faithfully worked in me as I have read through this book, and now I want to bring my heart completely before You and confess any area in which I have not fully accepted my husband for who he is. Please expose to me the parts of him that I am still trying to change, and may I give those areas of his life to You to smooth out or sift through as You will. Give me peace about leaving those matters in Your hands. Help me to continually let my husband know that I love him for who he is, not who I want him to become.

And God, please show me anything that might be festering in my heart for which I have not forgiven him and may I confess that to You, leaving that, too, in Your capable hands. Release my heart from any burdens, bitterness, or unmet expectations I still have of him so that he, too, can be released of the burden, bitterness, or sense of expectation he might feel from me.

Finally Lord Jesus, please help me to love my husband *as You* have loved me—showing him sacrificial love, protective love, and persevering love. And as I do that in Your strength, may You renew my love for him so that it, like Your mercy, is new every morning (Lamentations 3:22-23).

A Parting Encouragement

M y friend, thank you for wanting to know your man deeply. It thrills my heart that you have a desire to understand and affirm the man in your life. Here are some closing words of encouragement:

"We have the capacity for deep emotional experiences and can seem like a complicated and mixed bag of thoughts and feelings. We spend long hours taking care of our families and will fiercely defend and protect our children if we have to. We can multitask at work or at home when the situation calls for it, and we will sacrifice almost anything and everything to secure a good future for our children. We carry the pain when we see our family struggling or when a son or daughter is in trouble, and we lose sleep at night worrying about their decisions. We wrestle with the question of whether or not we've lived up to our spouses' expectations. We struggle with the fear that we'll let them down or disappoint them or our children somehow. And we need and desire real intimacy with others."

"That's right, Cindi. We women *are* so much like that," you may be saying. But I'm not talking about women here—rather, it's my husband, Hugh, speaking about men! Hugh continues:

"It's been said that men and women are from two completely different planets. But the fact is we're made from the same stuff (see Genesis 2:21-23), making us more alike than maybe we'd care to admit. The truth of the matter is that men are not from Mars and women are not from Venus. Men are from Earth, created from the dust of the ground in a Middle Eastern garden called Eden. And women are taken from the very flesh and bone of men."

I (Cindi) asked Hugh to give you a closing send-off to encourage your hearts. And I hope you are as encouraged as I am to remember that we—both male and female—are made in God's image, and that with His help, we can mirror His heart and attributes. As Scripture says, the first wife was taken from the side of her husband.

And you, in marriage, are brought to the side of *your* husband. Stay there. Live there. Walk alongside him and encourage him. You are the only woman on earth who has been given the privilege of helping, affirming, and inspiring him as a wife. So do what only *you* can do, pleasing God and touching your husband's soul. And do it well!

Recommended Resources

Helper by Design: God's Perfect Plan for Women in Marriage by Elyse Fitzpatrick (Chicago: Moody, 2003).

The Husband Project: 21 Days of Loving Your Man—On Purpose and with a Plan by Kathi Lipp (Eugene, OR: Harvest House, 2009).

Sacred Influence: How God Uses Wives to Shape the Souls of Their Husbands by Gary Thomas (Grand Rapids: Zondervan, 2006).

Romancing Your Husband: Enjoying a Passionate Life Together by Debra White Smith (Eugene, OR: Harvest House Publishers, 2002).

How to Get Your Husband to Talk to You by Nancy Cobb and Connie Grigsby (Sisters, OR: Multnomah, 2001).

6 Secrets to a Lasting Love by Dr. Gary and Barbara Rosberg (Carol Stream, IL: Tyndale, 2006).

Cinderella Meets the Caveman by Dr. David E. Clarke (Eugene, OR: Harvest House, 2007).

The Five Love Languages by Gary Chapman (Chicago: Northfield, 1995).

Notes

1. Gary Thomas, *Sacred Influence* (Grand Rapids: Zondervan, 2006), p. 85.

2. NASB.

3. Elisabeth Elliot, *Let Me Be a Woman* (Wheaton, IL: Tyndale, 1976), p. 78.

4. Elliot, p. 83.

5. According to a study published in the February 2004 issue of *Sex Roles: A Journal of Research*, male and female subjects were equally likely to express feelings of sympathy or lend support to friends, but often the circumstances surrounding the outward expression of emotion are highly dependent on the context, such as whether the subject is being watched by onlookers.

6. Source: http://www.speechmastery.com/gender-differences-in-communication.html.

7. *Letting God Meet Your Emotional Needs* (Eugene, OR: Harvest House, 2000), is available through Cindi's Web site at www.StrengthForTheSoul.com.

8. NASB.

9. Robert Jeffress, *Say Goodbye to Regret* (Sisters, OR: Multnomah, 1998), p. 41.

10. Elyse Fitzpatrick, *Helper by Design* (Chicago: Moody, 2003) pp. 36-37.

11. Dr. Gary and Barbara Rosberg, *6 Secrets to a Lasting Love* (Carol Stream, IL: Tyndale House, 2006), p. 187.

12. Rosberg, p. 187.

13. Fitzpatrick, p. 49.

14. Ephesians 4:29 NASB, emphasis added.

15. The Message.

16. The Message.

17. NASB, emphasis added.

18. The Bible's Song of Solomon is introduced as the "Song of Songs" in chapter 1, verse 1.

19. This quote was taken from an article called "Five Keys to Your Man's Inner Heart," which is based on the book *Simply Romantic Secrets* by Dennis Rainey. This article is available for viewing in the article archives at www.FamilyLife.com.

20. Thomas, p. 85.

21. NASB, emphasis added.

22. Fitzpatrick, p. 152.

23. Financial Peace University is a 13-week course by financial expert Dave Ramsey offered at various locations in the United States and online. He teaches individuals to achieve their goals by eliminating debt, saving for the future, and giving generously. For more information, see www.daveramsey.com.

24. Charles R. Swindoll, *Esther: A Woman of Strength and Dignity* (Nashville, TN: Word, 1997), p. 53.

25. NASB.

26. Proverbs 12:4; 14:1; 17:1; 19:13-14; 21:9,19; 25:24; 27:15.

27. 1 Corinthians 7:12-16.

28. Fitzpatrick, p. 135.

29. Amy Carmichael, *If* (Grand Rapids: Zondervan, 1980).

30. The Message.

31. 1 John 4:10-11 MSG.

Other Harvest House Books
by Cindi McMenamin

WHEN WOMEN WALK ALONE

Every woman—whether she's single or married—has walked
through the desert of loneliness. Whether you feel alone from
being single, facing challenging life situations, or from being the
spiritual head of your household, discover practical steps to finding support, transforming loneliness into spiritual growth, and
turning your alone times into life-changing encounters with God.

WHEN WOMEN WALK ALONE:
A 31-DAY DEVOTIONAL COMPANION

God is at your side, ready to speak to your heart. He knows your
every need, whether it be for guidance, encouragement, or comfort. Discover what it means to experience God's presence at all
times with the help of this 31-day devotional companion. And
face each day with a renewed sense of hope and fulfillment that
comes from resting in God's love. Can be used alone or as a companion volume to *When Women Walk Alone*.

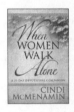

LETTING GOD MEET YOUR EMOTIONAL NEEDS

Do you long to have your emotional needs met, yet find that your
husband or those close to you cannot always help bring fulfillment to your life? Discover true intimacy with God in this book
that shows how to draw closer to the lover of your soul and find
that He can, indeed, meet your deepest emotional needs.

WHEN GOD PURSUES A WOMAN'S HEART

Within the heart of every woman is the desire to be cherished and
loved. Recapture the romance of a relationship with God as you
discover the many ways God loves you and pursues your heart
as your hero, provider, comforter, friend, valiant knight, loving
Daddy, perfect prince, and more.

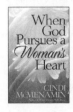

When Women Long for Rest

Women today are tired of feeling overwhelmed by all the demands on their lives and are longing for rest. They want to do more than just simplify or reorganize their lives. *When Women Long for Rest* is an invitation for women to find their quiet place at God's feet—a place where they can listen to Him, open their hearts to Him, and experience true rest.

When a Woman Discovers Her Dream

When it comes to living out the dream God has placed on your heart, do you shrug your shoulders and say, "It's too late…it's too far out of reach…it's too impossible for someone like me"? But you *can* live out that dream—no matter what your stage or place in life. Join Cindi as she shares how you can explore God's purposes for your life, make greater use of your special gifts, turn your dreams into reality, and become the masterpiece God designed you to be.

When You're Running on Empty

Are you feeling run down and ready to give up? If so, then you're probably running on empty. And you may feel as if the pressures and stress will never end. But there is a way out. Cindi shares from her own life and struggles many helpful and practical secrets about simplifying your priorities and obligations, rejuvenating yourself through God's Word, cultivating health habits that renew your energy, and learning to please God and not people.

Women on the Edge

We all have times when we find ourselves on the verge of frustration, despair, or even a meltdown. And we find ourselves at a crossroads: One path cries out for us to escape it all. The other calls us to persevere and lean on the Lord. Rather than merely survive, choose to abundantly thrive—by learning how to yield all control of your life to God, rest in His purpose and plan for your life, and enjoy the confidence of a heart wholly surrendered to Him.

When Couples Walk Together
(with Hugh McMenamin)

Are the demands of everyday life constantly pulling you and your spouse in different directions? If you've longed to rekindle the intimacy and companionship that first brought you together, join Hugh and Cindi McMenamin as they share 31 days of simple, creative, and fun ways you can draw closer together again. You'll find your marriage greatly enriched as you experience anew the joys of togetherness and unselfish love.

An Invitation to Write

How has God met you on this journey toward understanding and affirming the man in your life? And what kind of results have you seen as you have applied the biblical principles and practical insights in this book to your relationship with your husband? Cindi would love to hear from you and know how you've been ministered to or encouraged through her writing. You can contact her online at StrengthForTheSoul.com or write:

Cindi McMenamin
c/o Harvest House Publishers
990 Owen Loop North
Eugene, OR 97402-9173

For free resources to help strengthen your marriage or for information about Cindi's speaking ministry, see her website at www. StrengthForTheSoul.com.